The Generative AI Playbook

Create Viral Content, Boost Engagement, and Monetize Your Creativity

Oliver Grant

Table of Contents

Introduction

Introduction: The Future of Creativity is AI-Driven

Not too long ago, the idea of machines generating content that could rival human creativity seemed like science fiction. Today, it's reality. Artificial intelligence is not just transforming the way we create—it's redefining the entire landscape of content production, marketing, and digital entrepreneurship. What was once the exclusive domain of skilled writers, designers, and video producers is now accessible to anyone with an internet connection and the right AI tools.

You've probably heard the buzz—AI-generated articles going viral, AI-powered influencers dominating social media, and businesses leveraging AI for content that engages, converts, and sells. But here's the real question: How can you, as a creator, entrepreneur, or digital marketer, harness this AI revolution to build a thriving brand, captivate audiences, and generate income?

That's exactly what this book is about. "The Generative AI Playbook" is not just another book on artificial intelligence. It's your roadmap to mastering AI-powered content creation, optimizing engagement, and transforming your creativity into a scalable, revenue-generating machine. Whether you're a blogger looking to automate content, a marketer aiming to maximize engagement, or an entrepreneur seeking to monetize digital assets, this playbook gives you the strategies, tools, and ethical insights to stay ahead of the curve.

Why This Book Matters Now

The digital world is evolving at an unprecedented pace. Traditional content strategies alone are no longer enough to stand out. AI is leveling the playing field—allowing small creators to compete with industry giants and enabling businesses to scale faster than ever before. But here's the catch: AI is only as powerful as the person using it. Without a clear strategy, you risk creating generic, forgettable content that gets lost in the noise.

This book is designed to change that. **Inside, you'll learn:**

✓ How to use AI to generate high-impact content that resonates with your audience.

✓ The secrets behind viral AI-powered content and how to replicate it.

✓ Proven methods for monetizing AI-generated creations— from blog posts to digital products.

✓ The most effective AI tools for content creation, marketing, and brand growth.

✓ How to avoid common AI pitfalls—ensuring quality, originality, and ethical content production.

Who This Book is For

This book is for creators, entrepreneurs, marketers, and anyone who wants to leverage AI to maximize creativity and income. Whether you're a beginner exploring AI tools or an experienced content strategist looking for an edge, this playbook will help you navigate the AI-powered future with confidence.

AI is not here to replace creativity—it's here to amplify it. Those who understand how to use AI strategically will dominate the digital landscape, while those who ignore it will struggle to keep up. Which side of the future do you want to be on?

Welcome to the new era of AI-driven creativity. Let's get started.

Chapter 1: The AI Revolution in Content Creation

Introduction to Generative AI: What It Is and Why It Matters

The digital world is undergoing a transformation unlike anything we have seen before. Creativity, once thought to be a purely human domain, is now being enhanced—and in some cases, even generated—by artificial intelligence. From writing blog posts to producing music, generating art, and crafting entire video scripts, AI-powered tools are redefining how content is created, consumed, and monetized. This shift is not just a technological advancement; it is a revolution that is democratizing content creation, enabling individuals and businesses to produce at an unprecedented scale and efficiency.

Generative AI refers to artificial intelligence systems that can create new content based on existing data. Unlike traditional automation, which follows rigid instructions, generative AI can analyze patterns, understand context, and generate text, images, audio, and video that mimic human-like creativity. At the core of this innovation are advanced machine learning models such as OpenAI's GPT series, Google's Bard, and image-generation tools like MidJourney and DALL·E. These technologies rely on deep learning algorithms trained on vast amounts of data, allowing them to produce original and contextually relevant content.

The significance of generative AI extends far beyond automation. It is fundamentally changing how businesses market products, how influencers engage audiences, and how entrepreneurs build brands. With AI-driven content tools, a solo creator can generate professional-quality content at the speed and scale of an entire marketing team. Companies can personalize advertisements, optimize SEO strategies, and develop content calendars in a fraction of the time it would take using traditional methods. This acceleration is opening new doors for businesses of all sizes, from startups to global enterprises, by reducing costs, streamlining production, and increasing engagement.

One of the most remarkable aspects of generative AI is its ability to learn and adapt. Unlike static templates or predefined content generators, AI-driven platforms continuously refine their output based on user input and real-time data analysis. This makes AI an invaluable asset for content creators who want to remain agile in a fast-changing digital landscape. Social media trends, search engine algorithms, and audience preferences shift rapidly, and AI provides the ability to react and optimize content accordingly.

Despite its benefits, generative AI is not without challenges. Concerns over originality, bias, misinformation, and ethical considerations continue to shape the debate around its use. While AI can generate impressive results, it still lacks human intuition, emotional depth, and the ability to fully comprehend cultural nuances. This is why human oversight remains critical—AI should be seen as a tool that enhances creativity rather than replacing it. The best content is created when AI and human ingenuity work together, combining efficiency with originality.

Understanding generative AI is no longer optional for content creators and businesses looking to stay competitive. The tools and platforms powered by AI are evolving rapidly, and those who learn to leverage them effectively will have a significant advantage. This book is designed to help you navigate this revolution, equipping you with the knowledge and strategies needed to harness AI for content creation, audience engagement, and business growth.

Generative AI is not the future of content creation—it is the present. The question is no longer whether AI will impact creativity, but how you will choose to use it to your advantage. The rest of this book will provide you with the insights, tools, and techniques to not only keep up with this transformation but to thrive in it.

How AI is Reshaping Creativity Across Industries

The influence of artificial intelligence on creativity extends beyond content generation; it is fundamentally reshaping industries that rely on artistic expression, storytelling, and design. From marketing to film production, music composition, and even architecture, AI is redefining the boundaries of human ingenuity. By automating repetitive tasks, enhancing decision-making, and generating novel ideas, AI is not only making creative work more efficient but also expanding the possibilities of what can be created.

In the world of digital marketing, AI has revolutionized content personalization and audience targeting. Businesses can now use AI-driven tools to analyze consumer behavior, predict engagement trends, and generate customized ad copy tailored to specific audiences. AI-powered chatbots, social media management platforms, and predictive analytics have streamlined marketing strategies, making them more data-driven and effective. Copywriting tools like Jasper and Copy.ai allow marketers to produce compelling email campaigns, blog posts, and product descriptions at scale, ensuring that content remains fresh and optimized for conversion.

The film and entertainment industry has also embraced AI-driven creativity. Filmmakers and video editors use AI to automate editing, enhance special effects, and even generate deepfake technology for seamless character integration. AI-assisted scriptwriting tools analyze story structures and audience preferences to help screenwriters craft more engaging narratives. Video platforms such as Runway ML offer AI-powered tools for generating realistic visual effects, saving studios countless hours in production. AI-generated voice synthesis has also paved the way for dubbing, voice-overs, and even creating entirely new synthetic voices for animated films and virtual assistants.

The music industry is experiencing a similar transformation, with AI composing melodies, generating harmonies, and even mimicking the styles of legendary artists. AI platforms like AIVA and OpenAI's MuseNet allow musicians to experiment with different genres and structures, accelerating the songwriting process. AI-powered recommendation systems on platforms like Spotify and Apple Music use machine learning to predict user preferences and curate playlists, fundamentally altering the way audiences discover and consume music. Some artists have even collaborated with AI to co-create songs, using algorithms to generate unique soundscapes that blend human creativity with machine intelligence.

In visual arts and design, AI-generated images and illustrations have sparked both excitement and controversy. Programs like MidJourney, DALL·E, and Stable Diffusion can produce breathtaking artwork from simple text prompts, challenging traditional notions of artistic creation. Graphic designers now use AI to generate logos, layout templates, and branding materials with unprecedented speed. While some critics argue that AI-generated art diminishes the value of human craftsmanship, others see it as an opportunity to push creative boundaries and explore new forms of digital expression. AI-assisted design tools such as Adobe Sensei and Canva's AI-powered features allow designers to automate mundane tasks, refine compositions, and focus on higher-level creative decision-making.

Even architecture and product design are being reshaped by AI. Architects use AI-powered generative design software to optimize building structures, analyze environmental impact, and enhance efficiency in urban planning. AI algorithms assist in creating more sustainable and functional spaces, taking into account factors such as climate, material efficiency, and human ergonomics. In product design, AI-driven prototyping tools enable designers to test multiple iterations rapidly, identifying the best configurations before physical production begins.

AI's role in creative industries is not about replacing human artists, writers, or designers—it is about augmenting their capabilities. While AI can generate ideas, structure content, and optimize workflows, it still lacks the emotional depth, intuition, and originality that define human creativity. The future of creative work will be shaped by those who learn to harness AI as a collaborator, using its capabilities to enhance their artistic vision rather than replace it.

As AI continues to evolve, the challenge for creative professionals is not whether AI will change their industries, but how they can adapt and leverage its potential to unlock new opportunities. Those who embrace AI as a creative partner will find themselves at the forefront of innovation, leading industries into an era where human ingenuity and machine intelligence work hand in hand to redefine what is possible.

Breaking Down the Hype: What AI Can and Can't Do

Artificial intelligence has been hailed as a revolutionary force capable of transforming nearly every aspect of modern life, including content creation, marketing, and digital entrepreneurship. While AI's capabilities are undeniably impressive, much of the discourse surrounding it is clouded by exaggerated claims and unrealistic expectations. To fully harness the potential of AI, it is essential to distinguish between what AI can genuinely achieve and where its limitations lie. Understanding these distinctions prevents overreliance on automation and ensures that AI remains a powerful tool rather than a crutch.

One of AI's most significant strengths is its ability to process and generate content at an unprecedented scale. AI models like ChatGPT, Jasper, and Copy.ai can produce well-structured blog posts, social media captions, marketing emails, and even poetry within seconds. These tools enable businesses and creators to accelerate their content production, freeing up valuable time for strategic planning and engagement. AI is also highly effective at data analysis, identifying patterns in consumer behavior, optimizing ad campaigns, and tailoring content to specific audiences. By leveraging machine learning, AI-driven platforms can predict which types of content will perform best, maximizing reach and engagement.

AI's ability to enhance creativity extends beyond writing. It can generate images, compose music, edit videos, and even assist in film production. Tools like MidJourney and DALL·E create high-quality visuals based on text prompts, allowing designers and marketers to produce professional-grade graphics with minimal effort. In the music industry, AI-powered platforms such as AIVA and MuseNet help composers generate melodies and harmonies, streamlining the creative process. In video production, AI-driven editing software can automatically enhance footage, adjust lighting, and create dynamic cuts based on pacing and audience preferences. These capabilities demonstrate AI's potential as a powerful assistant that enhances efficiency and creativity across multiple disciplines.

Despite these advancements, AI remains fundamentally limited in several key areas. While it can generate impressive content, it lacks true originality, emotional depth, and lived experience. AI models operate by analyzing existing data and predicting the most statistically relevant responses, meaning they do not create content from genuine inspiration or personal insight. As a result, AI-generated content can sometimes feel formulaic, lacking the unique voice and perspective that distinguish human creativity. This is particularly evident in storytelling, where AI struggles to craft deeply nuanced narratives with rich character development and emotional complexity.

Another major limitation of AI is its inability to exercise true critical thinking and independent judgment. AI can generate logical-sounding responses, but it does not possess real-world reasoning or contextual awareness. It cannot verify facts in real-time or discern misinformation from credible sources. This limitation means that AI-generated content must always be reviewed for accuracy, especially in fields where precision and factual integrity are critical, such as journalism, medical writing, and legal documentation. Without human oversight, AI can unintentionally spread misleading or incorrect information, reinforcing the importance of responsible content curation.

Ethical concerns also arise when AI is used without proper transparency and accountability. Plagiarism, bias, and authenticity are ongoing challenges in AI-generated content. Since AI learns from existing datasets, it can inadvertently reproduce biased perspectives or replicate copyrighted material without proper attribution. Content creators who rely too heavily on AI-generated outputs risk facing credibility issues if their work lacks originality or fails to align with ethical standards. To mitigate these risks, AI should be used as a supplement rather than a replacement for human creativity, ensuring that content remains authentic and aligned with ethical guidelines.

Another significant challenge is AI's dependency on user input. While AI can generate content based on prompts, it lacks the intuition to understand abstract or complex ideas without clear direction. Poorly written prompts can result in generic or irrelevant responses, requiring users to refine their inputs multiple times to achieve satisfactory results. This means that AI is not a "set-and-forget" tool but rather a dynamic assistant that requires careful guidance and iterative refinement.

Ultimately, AI's role in content creation is best understood as an enabler rather than a creator in its own right. It can generate ideas, automate processes, and enhance productivity, but it cannot replace human creativity, emotional intelligence, or strategic thinking. The most successful AI-powered content creators are those who strike a balance—leveraging AI for efficiency while infusing their work with the personal touch, critical insight, and originality that only humans can provide.

By separating the hype from reality, it becomes clear that AI is a powerful tool, but it is not a magic wand. Those who understand its strengths and limitations will be best positioned to use it effectively, staying ahead of the curve while maintaining the authenticity and creativity that audiences value.

The Future of AI-Generated Content: Trends to Watch

Artificial intelligence is advancing at a rapid pace, reshaping the way content is created, distributed, and consumed. As AI technology continues to evolve, it is crucial for content creators, businesses, and marketers to stay ahead of emerging trends that will define the future of AI-generated content. These developments are not only changing workflows but also opening up new opportunities for innovation, monetization, and audience engagement.

One of the most significant trends in AI-generated content is the growing sophistication of personalization. AI-powered tools are becoming increasingly adept at tailoring content to individual preferences, behaviors, and engagement patterns. Personalized recommendations are already a staple of platforms like YouTube, Netflix, and Spotify, but the next phase will involve AI dynamically generating unique content experiences for each user. This could mean AI-crafted news articles that adjust their tone based on a reader's interests, custom video content that aligns with a viewer's watch history, or automated storytelling that adapts based on audience feedback. The ability to hyper-personalize content will revolutionize marketing, e-learning, and entertainment, making AI an indispensable tool for enhancing user engagement.

Another trend gaining momentum is the integration of AI with augmented reality (AR) and virtual reality (VR). AI-generated content is increasingly being used to create immersive experiences in gaming, education, and social interactions. AI-driven virtual influencers, synthetic brand ambassadors, and interactive AI-generated characters are becoming more prevalent, changing how businesses engage with consumers. In the near future, AI may be used to generate real-time dialogue for VR simulations, produce customized AR advertisements, or even create entire AI-generated virtual environments for training and storytelling. This shift will blur the lines between digital and physical interactions, making content consumption more interactive than ever.

AI-generated video content is another area poised for rapid growth. While AI-generated text and images have already seen widespread adoption, video production has remained a more complex challenge due to the intricacies of motion, emotion, and storytelling. However, advancements in AI-powered video creation tools, such as Runway ML and Synthesia, are making it easier to generate high-quality videos from simple text prompts. AI-driven deepfake technology, once seen as a novelty or ethical concern, is now being leveraged for more legitimate uses, such as personalized marketing, dubbing films into multiple languages, and creating synthetic news anchors. As AI video generation becomes more refined, it is likely to disrupt traditional media production by making high-quality video content more accessible to independent creators and small businesses.

Another emerging trend is the fusion of AI with voice synthesis and conversational AI. AI-generated voiceovers are already being used in audiobooks, podcasts, and digital assistants, but the future will bring even more lifelike and emotionally expressive AI voices. Companies like ElevenLabs and OpenAI are developing voice models that can mimic human intonation, accents, and emotions with remarkable accuracy. This will enable brands to create hyper-realistic virtual assistants, automate podcast production, and even allow authors to generate personalized audiobook narrations in their own voice without ever stepping into a recording studio. AI-driven voice interactions will also enhance chatbot experiences, making them more intuitive, responsive, and human-like.

Ethical AI content generation will also play a pivotal role in shaping the future. As AI-generated content becomes more prevalent, issues related to deepfake misuse, plagiarism, bias, and misinformation will become more pressing. Governments, tech companies, and content platforms will need to establish clearer regulations and best practices for AI-generated media.

Watermarking AI-generated content, improving transparency in AI-assisted work, and ensuring fair compensation for human creators whose work informs AI training data will become key discussions in the industry. As ethical concerns grow, responsible AI usage will become a differentiator for brands and creators who prioritize authenticity and integrity.

The rise of AI co-creativity is another trend that will redefine how AI and human creators collaborate. Rather than replacing human creativity, AI is increasingly being positioned as a creative partner, offering ideas, refining drafts, and assisting in brainstorming sessions. AI-assisted writing tools will become more advanced, allowing authors to outline books, generate character dialogue, and even suggest plot twists. In music, AI will continue to support composers by generating melodies, harmonies, and instrumental arrangements that artists can refine into finished compositions. The same applies to graphic design and digital art, where AI will help artists by automating repetitive tasks while leaving room for human expression and interpretation.

AI-driven content monetization will also see new opportunities emerge. As AI-generated content floods digital platforms, creators will need to differentiate themselves by offering premium, exclusive, or interactive experiences. Subscription-based AI-generated newsletters, AI-powered coaching programs, and pay-per-use AI content generation services could become new revenue streams. Additionally, blockchain and NFT technology may intersect with AI-generated content, allowing creators to establish ownership, track usage, and monetize digital assets in innovative ways.

The future of AI-generated content is not just about automation—it is about augmentation. AI is evolving from a simple content generator into an intelligent assistant that enhances creativity, personalizes experiences, and expands the possibilities of storytelling, marketing, and media production. Those who embrace AI as a tool rather than fear it as a replacement will be best positioned to thrive in this rapidly changing landscape. The coming years will see AI take a central role in content creation, not as a competitor to human creativity, but as a powerful collaborator in shaping the future of digital expression.

Chapter 2: The Viral Formula – How AI Can Predict and Generate Trending Content

Understanding the Science of Virality

Virality is not accidental. Behind every trending video, meme, or social media post lies a pattern—an underlying formula that captures attention, sparks emotions, and compels people to share. While traditional marketers have spent decades analyzing what makes content go viral, artificial intelligence has accelerated the process by identifying trends, analyzing engagement metrics, and predicting what will capture an audience's interest before it even happens. AI's ability to process vast amounts of data in real time has revolutionized the way creators and brands approach content strategy, making virality more systematic than ever before.

At its core, viral content taps into fundamental human psychology. Emotion is one of the most significant drivers of sharing behavior. Studies have shown that content that elicits strong emotions—whether it is joy, awe, surprise, anger, or fear—is far more likely to be shared than content that is neutral or purely informational. AI algorithms trained on social media interactions can detect emotional triggers in trending content, helping creators craft messages, headlines, and visuals that maximize engagement. By analyzing past viral hits, AI can determine what combination of words, images, and storytelling elements are most likely to provoke an emotional response.

Another key factor in virality is **relatability and social currency**. People share content that aligns with their identity, values, or social standing. AI tools powered by natural language processing and sentiment analysis can identify trending topics that resonate with specific demographics, allowing brands to tailor their messaging for maximum relatability. Whether it is a humorous meme, a motivational story, or an insightful industry trend, AI helps pinpoint what kind of content will make people want to engage and share.

Timeliness is also crucial. Viral content often capitalizes on trending news, cultural events, or seasonal moments that are top-of-mind for audiences. AI-driven trend analysis tools, such as Google Trends, BuzzSumo, and social media monitoring platforms, track emerging conversations and engagement spikes in real time. This allows creators to proactively jump on viral moments before they peak, increasing their chances of getting noticed. AI can also automate content adaptation, repurposing popular topics across different platforms in a way that optimizes them for each audience's preferences.

Visual impact plays a significant role in driving shares. Studies show that posts with compelling images, videos, and dynamic visuals receive far more engagement than text-only content. AI-powered design tools like Canva, DALL·E, and Runway ML can generate eye-catching graphics and video elements that enhance the shareability of a post. AI can even analyze visual aesthetics that are currently trending—whether it is a specific color scheme, typography style, or video editing effect—helping content creators produce materials that align with viral aesthetics.

The structure of content is another critical element in virality. Bite-sized, digestible formats such as listicles, infographics, and short-form videos tend to perform better than long, dense pieces. AI can help structure content in a way that optimizes readability, engagement, and retention. For example, AI-powered video editing software can identify the most engaging moments in a long video and automatically create short clips optimized for TikTok, Instagram Reels, or YouTube Shorts.

Similarly, AI-assisted writing tools can generate compelling headlines and introductions that immediately hook the audience, increasing the likelihood of clicks and shares.

Predictive analytics is where AI truly excels in unlocking virality. Instead of waiting for content to go viral organically, AI can analyze millions of data points—such as user engagement, click-through rates, and sharing behavior—to forecast which topics and formats have the highest chance of gaining traction. Platforms like TikTok, YouTube, and Twitter already use AI-driven recommendation algorithms to push high-engagement content to wider audiences. By leveraging AI insights, content creators can fine-tune their posts before publishing, ensuring they align with what is most likely to gain traction.

Virality is no longer just about luck. AI has turned it into a science, providing creators with data-driven strategies to maximize their reach and engagement. By understanding the psychology of sharing, leveraging AI's predictive power, and crafting content optimized for trends, creators and businesses can systematically increase their chances of going viral. The future of content marketing will be dominated by those who can combine AI's analytical capabilities with human creativity, ensuring that every piece of content is not just engaging but engineered for mass appeal.

Using AI to Analyze and Predict Viral Trends

The ability to predict viral trends before they reach peak popularity has become a game-changer in content creation and digital marketing. AI-driven analytics and machine learning algorithms are now capable of identifying emerging trends, analyzing engagement patterns, and forecasting what type of content is most likely to capture audience attention. Instead of relying on intuition or hindsight, creators and brands can use AI to strategically craft content that aligns with the next big trend, increasing their chances of achieving viral success.

AI trend analysis begins with **real-time data tracking**. Machine learning algorithms monitor millions of data points across social media platforms, search engines, and news websites to detect rising topics before they gain widespread attention. AI-powered tools like Google Trends, BuzzSumo, and TrendSpottr analyze search queries, hashtag movements, and social media engagement to highlight subjects that are rapidly gaining traction. These insights allow content creators to proactively produce material that capitalizes on the momentum of an emerging trend rather than reacting to it after it peaks.

Sentiment analysis plays a critical role in predicting virality. AI models use natural language processing (NLP) to scan online discussions, comments, and reviews to gauge public sentiment toward a specific topic. By identifying whether a trend is generating positive enthusiasm or sparking controversy, AI can help content creators determine the best angle to approach the subject. Brands can use sentiment analysis to shape their messaging, ensuring that their content resonates with audience emotions while avoiding potential backlash.

AI also analyzes **engagement patterns and user behavior** to forecast which types of content formats and styles are most likely to perform well. By examining past viral posts, AI can identify common elements such as video length, storytelling structure, emotional triggers, and visual aesthetics that contributed to high engagement rates. AI-powered content recommendation systems, like those used by YouTube, TikTok, and Instagram, leverage these insights to push trending content to a wider audience. By understanding these patterns, creators can optimize their own content strategies, increasing their likelihood of being featured on algorithm-driven discovery feeds.

Another powerful application of AI in trend prediction is **predictive analytics for social media virality**. AI tools analyze historical data on engagement spikes, audience demographics, and content performance to predict the best times to post and the most effective distribution channels. Platforms like Hootsuite, Sprout Social, and HubSpot use AI to provide optimal posting schedules and suggest the best formats for each platform. This ensures that content reaches its target audience at the right time, maximizing visibility and shareability.

AI-generated insights also extend beyond text and social media. In visual content creation, AI analyzes trending colors, design patterns, and imagery styles that are resonating with audiences. Tools like DALL·E and MidJourney generate visuals that align with emerging artistic trends, allowing designers and marketers to stay ahead of shifting aesthetic preferences. Similarly, AI-driven video editing tools can suggest the most engaging clips, transitions, and effects to enhance video performance based on trends identified from high-performing content across platforms.

The rise of **AI-powered trend prediction** is transforming the way businesses and content creators approach marketing. Instead of guessing what might work, AI enables a data-driven strategy that enhances precision, reduces trial and error, and increases the likelihood of viral success. By continuously learning from evolving audience behavior and engagement patterns, AI helps creators refine their approach, ensuring that their content remains relevant and ahead of the competition.

As AI continues to advance, its predictive capabilities will become even more refined, making it an indispensable tool for digital creators and marketers. Those who embrace AI-powered trend analysis will have a competitive edge, producing content that not only aligns with current interests but also anticipates what audiences will be looking for next. The future of viral content will belong to those who understand how to blend AI-driven insights with human creativity, ensuring that every post, video, or campaign is optimized for maximum impact.

How to Craft AI-Powered Headlines, Hooks, and Storylines

The effectiveness of content often hinges on its ability to grab attention within seconds. Whether it is a blog post, video, social media caption, or email subject line, the right headline and hook determine whether audiences engage or scroll past. AI-powered tools are revolutionizing how content creators craft compelling headlines, hooks, and storylines by analyzing engagement data, predicting audience reactions, and optimizing for virality. With AI, creators can craft content that not only captures attention but also maintains interest and drives action.

AI-powered headline generation relies on data-driven optimization. AI tools like Jasper, Copy.ai, and Writesonic analyze high-performing headlines across various platforms and generate suggestions tailored to specific industries, audiences, and content types. These tools break down what makes headlines effective, incorporating elements such as power words, urgency, emotional appeal, and curiosity gaps. For example, an AI-generated headline for a marketing article might transform a generic title like "How to Improve Your Sales" into "The Secret Sales Hack That Boosted Revenue by 300% in 30 Days." By analyzing past successful headlines, AI ensures that content titles align with patterns that have a proven track record of high engagement.

The hook is the next crucial component in capturing audience attention. AI analyzes thousands of high-performing introductions and first sentences to determine what keeps readers, viewers, and listeners engaged. AI-driven content assistants help craft opening lines that establish intrigue, create an emotional connection, or introduce a problem that the audience wants to see resolved. For example, instead of a standard opening like "Social media marketing is important for businesses," an AI-optimized hook might read, "Your competitors are stealing your customers on social media—here's how you can take them back." AI tools ensure that hooks are concise, impactful, and structured to draw audiences into the content immediately.

Storyline structuring is another area where AI is transforming content creation. AI tools analyze storytelling frameworks such as the hero's journey, problem-solution narrative, and emotional arcs to help creators develop compelling storylines that keep audiences engaged. AI-generated outlines help structure articles, scripts, and marketing copy by suggesting key turning points, tension-building elements, and resolutions that resonate with audiences. For instance, an AI-powered tool might suggest a storyline that starts with a personal struggle, transitions into discovery and experimentation, and concludes with a breakthrough or transformation. This approach ensures that narratives follow proven engagement models, increasing their likelihood of retention and shareability.

Another advantage of AI in crafting headlines, hooks, and storylines is its ability to personalize content for different audiences. AI-driven A/B testing tools generate multiple variations of headlines and introductions, analyzing which versions perform best based on click-through rates and engagement metrics. This allows content creators to optimize messaging for different platforms, demographics, and user behaviors. A headline that works well on LinkedIn may need a different tone on Twitter or Instagram, and AI can tailor messaging accordingly to maximize impact across various channels.

AI also enhances creativity by suggesting unexpected angles, unique perspectives, and alternative phrasings. By analyzing large datasets of trending topics and popular storytelling formats, AI can propose new ways to frame content that might not be immediately obvious to human creators. This prevents content from becoming repetitive or predictable, ensuring that headlines, hooks, and storylines stand out in an oversaturated digital landscape.

While AI can generate high-performing headlines and hooks, human intuition remains essential in refining and personalizing content. AI provides data-driven insights, but human creativity adds authenticity, emotion, and cultural nuance that AI cannot fully replicate. The best approach is to use AI as a powerful assistant—leveraging its analytical capabilities while maintaining a human touch that makes content feel personal and engaging.

The rise of AI in content creation is not just about automation but about enhancement. AI helps creators craft headlines that stop the scroll, hooks that pull readers in, and storylines that keep them engaged until the very end. Those who integrate AI-powered tools into their content strategy will gain a competitive edge, ensuring that every piece of content is optimized for maximum impact, engagement, and shareability.

Case Studies: How AI-Generated Content Went Viral

Artificial intelligence has already played a major role in creating viral content across various platforms, demonstrating its ability to engage audiences, spark conversations, and drive massive traffic. By analyzing patterns, optimizing messaging, and leveraging real-time data, AI has helped creators, businesses, and influencers craft content that captures attention and spreads rapidly. Examining real-world examples of AI-driven viral success provides insight into how content creators can replicate these strategies and maximize their reach.

One of the most well-known cases of AI-generated content going viral is the emergence of AI-created artwork. Platforms like MidJourney and DALL·E have enabled users to generate stunning, hyper-realistic images from simple text prompts, leading to massive engagement on social media. One viral instance occurred when an AI-generated painting titled "Théâtre D'opéra Spatial" won first place in a digital art competition at the Colorado State Fair. The controversy surrounding whether AI-generated art should be considered true creativity sparked widespread debate, resulting in millions of shares, discussions, and media coverage. This case demonstrates how AI-generated content can go viral by tapping into cultural and ethical conversations that capture public interest.

Another major AI-driven viral success story comes from Buzzfeed's AI-generated quizzes. By leveraging AI to create highly personalized and engaging quiz experiences, Buzzfeed significantly increased user interaction and shareability. AI-powered quizzes that predict a person's personality type, future profession, or celebrity look-alike consistently gain high engagement rates because they trigger curiosity and encourage social sharing. These AI-driven quizzes highlight how customization and interactivity enhance content virality, making audiences more likely to engage and spread the content.

AI-powered video content has also seen explosive viral success. A notable example is how TikTok influencers have used AI-generated voiceovers and deepfake technology to create engaging, humorous, or surreal videos. One of the most famous instances involved AI-generated deepfake videos of celebrities, such as Tom Cruise, where the hyper-realistic nature of the AI-assisted content captured millions of views. The virality of these videos was driven by their novelty and the seamless integration of AI in entertainment, sparking widespread conversation about the ethical implications and possibilities of AI-generated media.

In the music industry, AI-generated songs have gone viral by blending human creativity with machine intelligence. The most striking example occurred when an AI-generated song mimicking the voices of Drake and The Weeknd was uploaded to streaming platforms, fooling millions of listeners before being removed for copyright concerns. The song gained millions of streams within days, sparking industry-wide debates about the future of AI in music production. This case illustrates how AI can create viral content by producing hyper-realistic imitations of popular artists, raising questions about authorship, originality, and monetization in the digital age.

Marketing campaigns powered by AI have also demonstrated viral potential. A prime example is the AI-generated script for Lexus's commercial, which was written entirely by AI after analyzing decades of award-winning advertisements. The AI-crafted ad, titled "Driven by Intuition," incorporated emotional storytelling elements identified as successful in previous campaigns. The commercial's unique origin story attracted global media attention, resulting in millions of views and discussions about the future of AI in advertising. This case shows how AI-generated content can go viral by offering a novel approach to a traditional format, sparking curiosity and engagement.

AI-powered social media bots have also demonstrated the ability to generate viral content by participating in trending conversations. The AI-driven Twitter account "DeepDrumpf," which was trained on Donald Trump's speech patterns, went viral for generating eerily accurate tweets mimicking the former president's style. By leveraging AI's ability to analyze linguistic patterns and generate contextually relevant responses, the bot gained massive engagement, sparking discussions on the potential of AI-generated personas in digital communication. This case highlights how AI can create viral content by imitating influential figures and engaging in real-time discussions.

These examples illustrate that AI-generated content can achieve virality by capitalizing on novelty, personalization, controversy, and entertainment value. Whether through AI-generated visuals, interactive experiences, deepfake videos, or automated storytelling, AI is proving to be a powerful tool for creating highly shareable content. The key to success lies in understanding audience psychology, leveraging AI's analytical capabilities, and combining machine-generated insights with human creativity to produce content that resonates, surprises, and engages.

Chapter 3: AI-Powered Content Creation: From Idea to Execution

Generating Blog Posts, Articles, and SEO-Optimized Content

AI has transformed the way content is created, making it possible to generate high-quality blog posts, articles, and SEO-driven content in a fraction of the time it would take using traditional methods. With the ability to analyze vast amounts of data, predict audience preferences, and optimize for search engines, AI-powered writing tools have become indispensable for content creators, marketers, and businesses looking to scale their content strategy efficiently.

The process of AI-powered content generation begins with topic ideation. AI tools analyze trending topics, search queries, and audience engagement patterns to suggest high-performing content ideas. Platforms like Surfer SEO, SEMrush, and BuzzSumo use data-driven insights to identify what users are searching for and which topics are gaining traction. This eliminates the guesswork in content planning, allowing creators to focus on subjects that have a high likelihood of attracting traffic and engagement. AI can also generate content briefs that outline key subtopics, recommended keywords, and ideal word counts based on competitor analysis.

Once a topic is selected, AI writing assistants like ChatGPT, Jasper, and Copy.ai can generate well-structured blog posts and articles with minimal input. These tools leverage natural language processing (NLP) to create coherent, informative, and engaging content that mimics human writing. AI-powered platforms can produce long-form content in multiple formats, including how-to guides, listicles, case studies, and opinion pieces, allowing creators to tailor their content strategy to different audience preferences. AI writing tools also ensure consistency in tone and style, making them particularly useful for businesses that need to maintain a unified brand voice across multiple pieces of content.

SEO optimization is another area where AI excels. AI-driven tools analyze search engine algorithms to recommend keyword placements, meta descriptions, and internal linking strategies that improve search rankings. AI-powered writing platforms like Clearscope and Frase compare content against top-ranking articles and suggest optimizations that increase the likelihood of appearing on the first page of search results. AI also assists in crafting compelling headlines and meta tags that drive higher click-through rates, ensuring that content is not only well-written but also discoverable.

Beyond text generation, AI enhances readability and engagement by optimizing sentence structure, word choice, and formatting. AI tools like Grammarly and Hemingway Editor refine content by eliminating redundancies, improving clarity, and suggesting more concise phrasing. Readability scores generated by AI help writers tailor their content to specific audience demographics, ensuring that information is presented in a way that is accessible and engaging.

AI-generated content is also dynamic, allowing for real-time updates and personalization. AI-powered dynamic content platforms can tailor blog posts based on user behavior, geographic location, or browsing history. This means that a single article can be adjusted to appeal to different audiences without requiring manual rewrites. Personalization enhances user engagement, as readers receive content that feels more relevant to their interests and needs.

While AI-generated content offers efficiency and scalability, human oversight remains essential. AI tools provide a strong foundation, but they lack the ability to inject personal experiences, emotional depth, and unique storytelling elements that resonate on a deeper level. The most effective approach is to use AI as a collaborator rather than a replacement, allowing human creativity to refine and enhance AI-generated drafts. This ensures that content maintains authenticity, originality, and credibility while benefiting from AI-driven optimization.

AI-powered content creation is no longer a futuristic concept but a reality that is transforming how blog posts, articles, and SEO-driven content are produced. By leveraging AI for idea generation, writing, and optimization, content creators can streamline their workflows, improve search visibility, and maintain a consistent publishing schedule without compromising quality. As AI technology continues to evolve, those who embrace its capabilities while balancing it with human creativity will have a significant advantage in the competitive digital landscape.

AI in Video Content: Scriptwriting and Video Production

Artificial intelligence is revolutionizing video content creation, from generating compelling scripts to automating the production process. AI-powered tools are streamlining the way videos are conceptualized, written, edited, and optimized for engagement, making high-quality content accessible to creators of all skill levels. Whether used for YouTube videos, marketing campaigns, or entertainment productions, AI is enhancing efficiency and creativity in video storytelling.

AI-driven scriptwriting tools are changing the way video content is planned and structured. Platforms like ChatGPT, Jasper, and Sudowrite assist in developing compelling narratives, dialogue, and scene structures based on data-driven storytelling principles. AI analyzes successful video formats and audience engagement patterns to suggest script structures that maximize watch time and retention. It can generate scripts for different styles of content, including educational videos, advertisements, short films, and social media reels, ensuring that the script is aligned with the platform and target audience. AI-assisted scriptwriting also helps in brainstorming creative angles, refining tone and pacing, and ensuring consistency throughout the narrative.

In video production, AI-powered tools are automating editing and enhancing post-production processes. Software like Runway ML, Magisto, and Adobe Sensei use machine learning to analyze footage, identify key moments, and edit videos seamlessly. AI can automatically trim unnecessary content, apply transitions, enhance lighting and color grading, and synchronize video with background music. These capabilities reduce the time and effort required for manual editing, allowing creators to focus on storytelling rather than technical adjustments. AI-driven video generation platforms like Synthesia and Pictory take automation a step further by creating full-length videos using AI-generated avatars, voiceovers, and animations, making it possible to produce professional-quality content without a traditional production team.

AI also plays a critical role in enhancing video engagement and distribution. AI-powered recommendation systems, such as those used by YouTube and TikTok, analyze user preferences and viewing habits to suggest the most relevant content. Creators can leverage AI tools to optimize thumbnails, titles, and descriptions based on predictive engagement analysis. AI-generated captions and translations improve accessibility, ensuring that videos reach a wider audience by supporting multiple languages and making content more inclusive for viewers with hearing impairments.

Another significant advancement in AI-driven video production is deepfake technology and AI-generated actors. AI-powered face-swapping tools and voice synthesis technology allow for realistic character replication, making it possible to generate virtual influencers or recreate historical figures for storytelling purposes. While these innovations open new creative possibilities, they also raise ethical concerns regarding authenticity and misinformation, highlighting the need for responsible AI use in video production.

The integration of AI in video content creation is reshaping how videos are produced, optimized, and distributed. By automating scriptwriting, streamlining editing, and enhancing personalization, AI empowers creators to produce high-quality videos faster and more efficiently. As AI technology continues to advance, its role in video production will only expand, offering new opportunities for filmmakers, marketers, and digital creators to push the boundaries of storytelling and audience engagement.

Leveraging AI for Podcasting and Audio Content

AI is transforming podcasting and audio content creation by automating production, enhancing quality, and personalizing the listening experience. From generating scripts and editing recordings to creating AI-driven voiceovers and optimizing audience engagement, artificial intelligence is making high-quality audio content more accessible to creators at all levels. These advancements allow podcasters, marketers, and businesses to streamline their workflow, reduce production costs, and increase audience reach with minimal effort.

AI-powered scriptwriting tools are revolutionizing podcast content development. Platforms like ChatGPT, Jasper, and Descript assist in brainstorming episode ideas, structuring engaging scripts, and generating conversational dialogue. AI analyzes audience engagement data to suggest trending topics, optimize storytelling flow, and refine messaging to align with listener preferences. This helps podcasters create compelling narratives, improve pacing, and maintain consistency in tone across multiple episodes. AI also aids in generating interview questions and summarizing key discussion points, making preparation more efficient for hosts.

Voice synthesis technology is another groundbreaking AI application in podcasting. AI-powered voice generators like ElevenLabs, Murf, and Amazon Polly enable creators to produce realistic and natural-sounding voiceovers without the need for a human narrator. This is particularly useful for podcasters who want to scale their content without recording every episode themselves. AI-generated voices can be customized to match different tones, accents, and styles, allowing for multilingual podcasts or automated content updates. Some creators are even using AI to clone their own voices, making it possible to generate new podcast episodes without additional recording time.

AI-driven editing tools are streamlining the post-production process by automating tasks that traditionally require hours of manual work. Platforms like Descript, Adobe Podcast, and Auphonic use machine learning to remove background noise, adjust audio levels, and enhance clarity in real-time. AI can automatically detect and remove filler words, long pauses, and awkward speech patterns, making conversations sound more polished and professional. Advanced AI features also allow for automatic transcription, making it easier for creators to repurpose podcast episodes into blog posts, social media snippets, and SEO-friendly articles.

Personalization and audience engagement are also being improved through AI analytics. AI-powered platforms analyze listener behavior, track engagement metrics, and suggest content strategies to maximize reach. Spotify, Apple Podcasts, and other major streaming services use AI-driven recommendation engines to match podcasts with relevant audiences based on listening habits and preferences. Independent podcasters can leverage similar AI insights to optimize episode release schedules, refine marketing strategies, and tailor content to audience demographics. AI-generated metadata optimization also improves discoverability by suggesting the best keywords, descriptions, and tags to increase podcast rankings on search platforms.

AI is also being used to create interactive and dynamic audio experiences. AI chatbots and voice assistants enable listeners to engage with podcast content in new ways, such as asking follow-up questions, receiving personalized episode recommendations, or interacting with AI-generated co-hosts. These innovations are redefining how audiences consume audio content, making podcasts more immersive and engaging.

By leveraging AI for podcasting and audio content, creators can enhance production quality, automate repetitive tasks, and expand their reach more efficiently. As AI technology continues to evolve, its role in the podcasting industry will only grow, offering new opportunities for storytelling, audience engagement, and monetization. Those who embrace AI-driven tools will be well-positioned to stay ahead in the rapidly expanding world of digital audio content.

AI-Generated Images, Graphics, and Designs

Artificial intelligence is transforming visual content creation, enabling designers, marketers, and content creators to generate high-quality images, graphics, and designs faster and more efficiently than ever before. AI-powered tools are reshaping industries by automating design processes, enhancing creativity, and personalizing visual content based on audience preferences. Whether for branding, social media, product packaging, or digital art, AI is redefining the creative landscape by making professional-grade design accessible to everyone.

AI-driven image generation platforms like DALL·E, MidJourney, and Stable Diffusion can create stunning visuals from simple text prompts. These tools use deep learning models trained on vast datasets of artwork, photographs, and graphic designs to generate unique, high-resolution images tailored to specific styles and themes. From hyper-realistic landscapes to abstract digital art, AI allows creators to bring their visions to life without needing advanced design skills. Businesses and marketers leverage AI-generated visuals to produce engaging content for advertisements, presentations, and branding materials, reducing reliance on stock images and costly custom photography.

AI is also revolutionizing graphic design by streamlining the creation of logos, social media posts, and marketing materials. Platforms like Canva and Adobe Sensei integrate AI-driven design assistants that suggest optimal layouts, color schemes, and typography based on branding guidelines. AI-powered design generators allow users to produce professional-quality graphics with just a few clicks, making it easier for small businesses and independent creators to maintain a consistent and visually appealing brand identity. These tools also analyze engagement data to recommend design elements that align with current trends and audience preferences, ensuring that visuals are optimized for maximum impact.

Customization and personalization are key advantages of AI-generated design. AI algorithms analyze user behavior and preferences to create adaptive visuals that change based on audience demographics and engagement patterns. Dynamic ad creatives powered by AI adjust in real time to match user interests, increasing conversion rates and engagement. Personalized product packaging and branding materials can be generated using AI, allowing businesses to create unique experiences for different customer segments.

In web and UI/UX design, AI enhances efficiency by automating layout generation and optimizing user experiences. AI-driven platforms like Uizard and Framer use machine learning to convert sketches into fully functional website and app designs, reducing the time and effort required for development. AI-powered heatmaps analyze user interactions to predict which design elements will drive the most engagement, helping designers refine layouts for improved usability and conversion rates.

AI is also being integrated into video and animation design. AI-powered video generators like Runway ML and Synthesia create dynamic motion graphics and animated visuals without requiring complex editing skills. These tools enable marketers and content creators to produce engaging video content quickly, incorporating AI-generated animations, transitions, and effects that align with brand aesthetics. AI-assisted video enhancement tools automatically adjust lighting, color grading, and frame rates to improve the visual quality of footage.

While AI-generated designs offer speed and efficiency, human creativity remains essential in refining and directing AI outputs. AI serves as a powerful assistant, providing inspiration, automating repetitive tasks, and optimizing visuals for engagement, but designers must still apply their artistic judgment to ensure originality and emotional resonance. The most successful AI-powered designs come from a collaboration between machine intelligence and human creativity, combining data-driven insights with unique artistic expression.

As AI continues to evolve, its impact on visual content creation will expand, opening new possibilities for personalized, high-quality, and cost-effective design. Businesses, marketers, and artists who embrace AI-driven tools will gain a competitive edge, producing visually compelling content that captures attention and drives engagement in a rapidly changing digital landscape.

Chapter 4: Mastering AI-Driven Social Media Growth

Using AI for Personalized Social Media Engagement

Social media has become the backbone of digital marketing, and personalized engagement is the key to building a loyal audience. Artificial intelligence is transforming how brands, businesses, and influencers interact with their followers, allowing for deeper connections, tailored content, and data-driven strategies that increase engagement. AI-driven tools analyze user behavior, preferences, and real-time interactions to create highly personalized experiences that foster brand loyalty and drive conversions.

AI-powered chatbots and virtual assistants have revolutionized customer interaction on social platforms. Tools like ChatGPT-powered bots, ManyChat, and Drift can instantly respond to customer inquiries, recommend products, and guide users through purchasing decisions. Unlike traditional automated responses, AI chatbots use natural language processing to create conversational and human-like interactions, ensuring that customers feel heard and valued. These chatbots operate 24/7, allowing brands to provide instant support and maintain engagement even outside business hours.

Predictive analytics plays a crucial role in AI-driven social media personalization. AI tools analyze past interactions, comments, and engagement metrics to predict what type of content individual users are most likely to engage with. Platforms like Sprout Social and Hootsuite use AI to recommend the best posting times, ideal content formats, and trending hashtags to maximize visibility. By understanding what resonates with different audience segments, businesses can craft targeted campaigns that increase retention and drive more meaningful interactions.

AI-generated content recommendations help social media managers maintain a consistent and relevant posting strategy. AI tools analyze trending topics, competitor performance, and audience sentiment to suggest content ideas that align with current trends. Platforms like Lately and Cortex use machine learning to repurpose high-performing content, ensuring that brands maximize the value of their existing posts by adapting them for different platforms and audience segments. AI-driven tools can also optimize captions, emojis, and hashtags based on audience preferences, improving engagement rates without requiring manual testing.

AI enhances influencer marketing by identifying the most effective partnerships. AI-powered influencer analytics platforms like Heepsy and Upfluence analyze engagement rates, audience demographics, and content authenticity to match brands with influencers who align with their target market. These tools also detect fake followers and engagement manipulation, ensuring that businesses invest in genuine influencer relationships that yield real results. AI-driven sentiment analysis evaluates how audiences react to influencer content, helping brands refine their messaging and collaborations for maximum impact.

Personalized video and image content are becoming more important in social media engagement, and AI plays a key role in automating and optimizing these elements. AI-powered video editing tools like Runway ML and Magisto analyze viewer engagement data to create dynamic, high-impact videos tailored to specific audience preferences. AI-generated images and personalized GIFs enhance brand identity and increase shareability. Platforms like Canva and Adobe Sensei use AI to suggest visually appealing design elements, helping social media managers create stunning content quickly and efficiently.

Another significant impact of AI on social media engagement is sentiment analysis. AI tools like Brandwatch and MonkeyLearn monitor audience reactions, analyzing positive, neutral, and negative sentiments in real time. This enables brands to quickly adjust their messaging, respond to customer concerns, and capitalize on trending discussions. AI-driven insights also help businesses identify potential PR risks before they escalate, allowing for proactive reputation management.

By leveraging AI for personalized social media engagement, brands and influencers can create deeper connections with their audiences, optimize content for maximum impact, and automate repetitive tasks without sacrificing authenticity. AI-driven strategies ensure that every interaction is relevant, timely, and tailored to individual user preferences, ultimately leading to higher engagement, increased brand loyalty, and stronger online communities. As AI technology continues to advance, those who embrace AI-driven personalization will gain a competitive edge in the fast-evolving world of social media marketing.

How to Automate Posts While Keeping Them Authentic

Automation has become an essential tool for social media management, allowing businesses, influencers, and content creators to maintain a consistent presence without the need for constant manual posting. However, one of the biggest challenges of automation is ensuring that scheduled posts remain authentic, engaging, and personal rather than robotic or generic. AI-powered tools can streamline the content creation and scheduling process while preserving the human touch that makes social media interactions meaningful.

The first step in automating social media posts while maintaining authenticity is to develop a well-defined content strategy. AI-driven platforms like Hootsuite, Buffer, and Sprout Social allow users to schedule posts in advance, but the key is to ensure that these posts align with brand voice, audience interests, and current trends. Rather than simply queuing up generic content, AI-powered analytics can help determine the best times to post, the most effective formats, and the topics that resonate most with followers. By analyzing engagement metrics, AI ensures that automated content remains relevant and timely.

Using AI to generate captions and headlines can enhance efficiency, but adding a personal touch is essential to maintaining authenticity. AI writing assistants like Jasper and Copy.ai can suggest engaging copy based on past high-performing posts, but manual refinement is necessary to inject brand personality. A mix of AI-generated text and human editing ensures that content feels natural rather than overly polished or robotic. This approach allows businesses to scale content production without losing the voice that makes them unique.

Dynamic content adaptation is another way to automate posts while keeping them personal. AI tools analyze audience segments and adjust content accordingly, ensuring that different users receive messaging that speaks directly to their preferences. For example, AI-powered personalization engines can modify language, tone, or imagery based on demographic data, engagement history, and platform behavior. A fitness brand, for instance, might schedule different workout tips for beginners and advanced athletes, ensuring that each audience segment feels directly addressed.

Authenticity is also maintained through interactive and real-time engagement. While AI can handle content scheduling, it is crucial to combine automation with active audience interaction. Social media chatbots and automated responses can provide instant replies to inquiries, but personalized follow-ups and human-led conversations enhance trust and engagement. AI-powered tools can flag important comments or questions that require a more thoughtful response, ensuring that brands remain responsive without relying solely on automation.

Leveraging user-generated content (UGC) is another way to balance automation with authenticity. AI-driven tools can identify high-performing UGC, such as customer reviews, testimonials, or social media mentions, and integrate them into scheduled posts. Featuring real customer experiences and organic content from followers adds credibility and human connection, making automated posts feel less like corporate messaging and more like genuine community engagement.

AI-assisted A/B testing ensures that automated posts are continuously optimized while staying authentic. AI can analyze different variations of scheduled content, such as alternate captions, visuals, or hashtags, to determine which versions perform best. By monitoring engagement in real time, AI refines future scheduled posts to align more closely with audience preferences. This adaptive approach ensures that automated content remains dynamic rather than static, evolving based on real-time feedback.

One of the most effective ways to maintain authenticity in automated posts is to blend scheduled content with spontaneous, real-time updates. While AI can handle regular posting, brands should leave room for live interactions, breaking news, and behind-the-scenes content that showcases the human side of the brand. Posting real-time stories, responding to trending topics, or sharing personal experiences alongside scheduled posts creates a balance that keeps social media presence engaging and relatable.

By strategically integrating AI automation with human oversight, businesses and creators can maintain a consistent posting schedule without sacrificing authenticity. AI-driven tools help streamline content creation, optimize timing, and personalize messaging, but the key to success lies in blending automation with genuine engagement. The most effective social media strategies use AI as an assistant, not a replacement, ensuring that every post feels intentional, relevant, and truly connected to the audience.

AI Tools for Optimizing Captions, Hashtags, and Post Timing

Artificial intelligence has transformed social media marketing by optimizing key elements that drive engagement, including captions, hashtags, and post timing. AI-powered tools analyze vast amounts of data to generate compelling captions, identify the most effective hashtags, and determine the best times to post for maximum visibility. These capabilities enable businesses, influencers, and content creators to increase reach, improve engagement, and streamline their social media strategies with minimal manual effort.

AI-generated captions enhance engagement by crafting text that resonates with audiences while aligning with brand voice and platform-specific trends. Tools like Copy.ai, Jasper, and ChatGPT analyze audience sentiment, trending keywords, and successful past posts to generate captions that are attention-grabbing and highly shareable. AI can tailor captions for different tones, whether humorous, inspirational, informative, or persuasive, ensuring that content matches the intended message. Some AI tools also incorporate emotional triggers and storytelling techniques, increasing the likelihood of interaction. While AI generates captions efficiently, manual refinement helps maintain authenticity, ensuring that the messaging feels natural rather than automated.

Hashtag optimization is another area where AI significantly enhances social media performance. AI tools like Hashtagify, RiteTag, and Flick analyze trending hashtags, audience interests, and competitor strategies to recommend the best hashtags for each post. These platforms evaluate hashtag performance metrics such as reach, engagement rates, and saturation levels, allowing users to select a mix of popular and niche hashtags that maximize discoverability. AI also suggests dynamic hashtag strategies that adapt to evolving trends, ensuring that posts remain relevant in real-time conversations. By using AI-driven hashtag research, brands can expand their reach beyond their existing audience and improve content discoverability across multiple platforms.

Timing plays a crucial role in content performance, and AI tools optimize post scheduling by analyzing audience behavior patterns. Platforms like Hootsuite, Sprout Social, and Later use machine learning to determine the optimal posting times based on when followers are most active and engaged. AI evaluates historical engagement data, platform-specific algorithms, and industry benchmarks to recommend the best time slots for each post. By automating the scheduling process with AI insights, creators can ensure that their content is published when it has the highest potential for visibility and interaction.

AI-powered analytics continuously refine captions, hashtags, and post timing based on real-time performance data. These tools track engagement metrics such as likes, shares, comments, and click-through rates to identify what strategies are most effective. A/B testing capabilities allow users to experiment with different variations of captions and hashtags, helping them refine their approach for future posts. AI-driven analytics also provide predictive insights, enabling users to adjust their content strategy proactively rather than reactively.

Integrating AI tools into social media workflows helps streamline content creation, improve engagement, and maximize the impact of every post. By leveraging AI for captions, hashtags, and post timing, businesses and creators can optimize their social media presence without relying on guesswork. AI-powered insights ensure that content reaches the right audience at the right time with the right message, leading to increased visibility, higher engagement, and more effective brand growth.

Case Studies: Social Media Influencers Who Use AI Successfully

Artificial intelligence has become a powerful tool for social media influencers, enabling them to optimize content, engage audiences, and grow their personal brands more efficiently. AI-driven analytics, automation tools, and content-generation platforms have allowed influencers to refine their strategies, increase engagement, and stay ahead of trends. Examining real-world examples of influencers who have successfully integrated AI into their social media presence provides insight into how AI can be leveraged to enhance digital influence.

One of the most prominent examples is TikTok influencer Caryn Marjorie, who launched an AI-generated version of herself, "CarynAI." Using AI-driven voice synthesis and chatbot technology, she created a virtual companion for her followers, offering personalized interactions at scale. This AI-powered initiative allowed her to monetize engagement through a subscription-based chatbot, demonstrating how influencers can use AI to deepen audience relationships and create new revenue streams. By automating personalized interactions while maintaining her unique brand identity, she set a new precedent for AI-assisted influencer engagement.

Another example is YouTube creator Marques Brownlee, known for his tech reviews. Brownlee integrates AI tools to optimize video production, analyze trending topics, and enhance his content's SEO performance. By using AI-driven analytics, he identifies which tech products are generating the most interest, allowing him to create videos on subjects with high engagement potential. AI-powered transcription tools also help him generate captions and improve search rankings, ensuring his content reaches broader audiences. Through AI-assisted insights, he consistently produces high-quality videos that align with audience demand, maintaining his status as a top tech influencer.

On Instagram, fashion influencer Camila Coelho leverages AI-powered trend analysis and engagement metrics to refine her content strategy. AI tools help her predict upcoming fashion trends based on search queries, purchase behaviors, and engagement rates across social platforms. By integrating AI-driven image enhancement tools like Adobe Sensei, she optimizes her visuals to align with platform-specific aesthetics. Additionally, AI-powered audience segmentation tools allow her to personalize content for different demographic groups, ensuring maximum engagement. Her use of AI for data-driven content planning and visual optimization has contributed to her continued growth in the competitive fashion industry.

AI is also playing a role in fitness and wellness influencing. Chris Heria, a popular fitness YouTuber and entrepreneur, utilizes AI-driven personalization tools to enhance user engagement. His AI-powered fitness app tailors workout plans based on individual performance metrics, making the experience more interactive and data-driven. On social media, AI analytics help him optimize video titles, thumbnails, and descriptions, ensuring maximum visibility. AI-powered editing software streamlines his video production process, allowing him to publish high-quality content more frequently while maintaining authenticity.

In the beauty and lifestyle space, Michelle Phan has incorporated AI into her content and business strategy. By leveraging AI-driven beauty analysis tools, she provides personalized skincare and makeup recommendations to her audience. Her brand, EM Cosmetics, integrates AI-powered customer insights to predict which products will resonate most with her followers. On social media, she uses AI-driven chatbots to answer beauty-related questions, creating an interactive experience for her audience. Her use of AI has not only improved audience engagement but has also positioned her as an innovator in AI-driven influencer marketing.

These case studies highlight how AI is becoming an essential tool for influencers across various industries. By using AI for trend prediction, audience engagement, content optimization, and monetization, influencers can enhance their online presence while maintaining authenticity. The ability to leverage AI-driven insights allows influencers to stay ahead in the fast-evolving digital landscape, ensuring that their content remains relevant, engaging, and impactful. As AI technology continues to advance, more influencers will integrate AI into their strategies, further transforming the way digital influence is built and maintained.

Chapter 5: Monetizing AI-Generated Content: Profitable Strategies

AI-Driven Affiliate Marketing and Passive Income

Artificial intelligence has transformed affiliate marketing and passive income strategies by automating content creation, optimizing audience targeting, and improving conversion rates. AI-powered tools allow content creators, bloggers, and marketers to scale their affiliate marketing efforts with less manual effort while increasing efficiency and revenue potential. Whether through AI-generated blog posts, automated email campaigns, or AI-driven product recommendations, leveraging AI in affiliate marketing creates a powerful framework for generating passive income.

One of the most effective ways AI enhances affiliate marketing is through content automation. AI writing assistants like Jasper, Copy.ai, and ChatGPT can generate high-quality product reviews, comparison articles, and SEO-optimized blog posts in minutes. These AI tools analyze search trends and competitor content to ensure that affiliate-driven content ranks higher in search engine results. By continuously updating and refining content based on engagement metrics, AI ensures that affiliate pages remain relevant and competitive, leading to sustained organic traffic and conversions.

AI-driven chatbots and virtual assistants further streamline affiliate marketing by engaging potential customers and answering product-related questions in real time. AI-powered customer interaction tools like Drift and ManyChat can guide visitors through the buyer's journey, recommending products based on their interests and previous interactions. These AI-driven assistants increase conversion rates by providing a personalized shopping experience, making it more likely that users will click affiliate links and complete purchases.

AI also optimizes affiliate marketing through predictive analytics. AI-powered tools like Google Analytics, SEMrush, and HubSpot analyze user behavior to predict which products or services are most likely to convert. AI can identify which content formats, keywords, and promotional strategies generate the highest affiliate sales, allowing marketers to fine-tune their approach. By automating A/B testing, AI determines the most effective calls to action, email subject lines, and social media ads, maximizing ROI for affiliate campaigns.

Social media is another area where AI plays a crucial role in driving passive income through affiliate marketing. AI-powered scheduling tools like Hootsuite and Buffer analyze engagement patterns to determine the best times to post affiliate content. AI-generated hashtags, captions, and image recommendations enhance visibility and ensure that affiliate links reach the right audience. Platforms like TikTok and Instagram have seen a surge in AI-assisted influencer marketing, where AI tools help creators identify trending products, generate compelling promotional content, and optimize ad spending for maximum affiliate commissions.

Email marketing remains one of the most effective channels for affiliate marketing, and AI is making it even more powerful. AI-driven email platforms like Mailchimp and ActiveCampaign use machine learning to personalize email content based on user behavior and preferences. AI can segment audiences, automate follow-up sequences, and recommend affiliate products based on past interactions. Predictive analytics help determine which subscribers are most likely to convert, allowing marketers to focus efforts on high-value leads.

AI-generated video content is also changing the landscape of affiliate marketing. Tools like Synthesia and Runway ML enable creators to produce engaging video reviews, tutorials, and product demonstrations without extensive editing skills. AI-powered video optimization ensures that content is formatted correctly for platforms like YouTube and TikTok, increasing visibility and engagement. By incorporating AI-driven scripts and automated captions, affiliate marketers can create high-quality video content that drives traffic to their affiliate links.

AI-powered recommendation engines enhance passive income potential by dynamically suggesting affiliate products to users based on their browsing behavior. E-commerce giants like Amazon and Shopify already use AI to recommend products, and affiliate marketers can leverage similar AI-driven plugins to display personalized product suggestions on their websites. AI tools analyze purchase history, user intent, and engagement metrics to present affiliate offers most likely to convert, increasing commission earnings with minimal effort.

By leveraging AI-driven tools and automation strategies, affiliate marketers can create a scalable, passive income model that requires minimal ongoing management. AI's ability to analyze data, optimize content, and personalize user experiences makes it an invaluable asset in the world of affiliate marketing. Those who integrate AI into their affiliate marketing strategies will gain a competitive edge, maximizing their earning potential while minimizing manual effort. As AI technology continues to evolve, the opportunities for generating passive income through AI-driven affiliate marketing will only expand, offering content creators and entrepreneurs new ways to monetize their digital presence efficiently.

Selling AI-Generated Digital Products (Ebooks, Art, Templates)

AI has revolutionized digital product creation, allowing entrepreneurs, content creators, and designers to generate high-quality digital assets at scale. From AI-written ebooks to AI-generated artwork and customizable design templates, artificial intelligence enables individuals to create and sell products with minimal time and effort. By leveraging AI tools, sellers can automate content production, optimize for market demand, and generate passive income through digital sales platforms.

One of the most popular AI-driven digital products is ebooks. AI writing assistants like ChatGPT, Jasper, and Sudowrite can generate well-structured, engaging content on virtually any topic. Whether creating non-fiction guides, self-help books, business strategies, or fiction novels, AI enables authors to outline, draft, and refine ebooks in a fraction of the time it would take using traditional writing methods. AI-powered editing tools like Grammarly and Hemingway enhance readability and coherence, ensuring that the final product is polished and professional. Once created, AI-generated ebooks can be sold on platforms like Amazon Kindle Direct Publishing (KDP), Gumroad, and Shopify, providing a passive income stream for digital entrepreneurs.

AI-generated art has also become a lucrative market, with tools like MidJourney, DALL·E, and Stable Diffusion allowing creators to produce unique and visually stunning artwork with simple text prompts. These AI tools empower artists to generate custom illustrations, digital paintings, and concept designs that can be sold as prints, wallpapers, NFTs, or stock images. AI-generated art appeals to both businesses and consumers, with companies purchasing designs for branding and marketing purposes, while individuals seek unique visuals for personal use. Marketplaces like Etsy, Redbubble, and Adobe Stock provide platforms for selling AI-created digital art, offering a scalable way to monetize creative assets.

Design templates are another profitable AI-generated digital product. AI-powered design platforms like Canva, Adobe Sensei, and Looka allow users to create professional-grade templates for presentations, social media graphics, business cards, website layouts, and branding kits. Entrepreneurs can develop and sell editable templates that businesses, marketers, and content creators can customize for their own needs. These templates save buyers time while allowing sellers to generate ongoing revenue from a single digital product. AI-driven optimization tools can further enhance template effectiveness by analyzing design trends and recommending styles that align with current market demands.

AI-generated digital planners, journals, and workbooks are also in high demand. Productivity tools created with AI assistance can include goal-setting planners, habit trackers, and guided journals tailored to different niches such as business, wellness, and self-improvement. These digital products can be sold as downloadable PDFs on platforms like Gumroad, Etsy, or Sellfy, catering to individuals looking for structured resources to enhance their workflow and daily routines.

AI-powered music and sound effects are expanding the digital product market as well. Platforms like AIVA and Boomy allow creators to generate royalty-free music compositions that can be sold for commercial use in videos, podcasts, and advertisements. AI-generated sound effects and voiceovers are increasingly valuable in industries like gaming, film production, and content creation, opening up new monetization opportunities for those who leverage AI to produce high-quality audio assets.

Selling AI-generated digital products offers a scalable and cost-effective way to monetize creativity without the need for physical inventory or high production costs. By using AI tools to generate ebooks, artwork, design templates, and other digital assets, entrepreneurs can create a sustainable business model with minimal ongoing effort. The key to success lies in choosing high-demand products, optimizing them for specific target audiences, and leveraging digital marketplaces to maximize reach. As AI technology continues to evolve, the opportunities for selling AI-generated digital products will only expand, providing endless possibilities for content creators and digital entrepreneurs looking to generate passive income.

AI-Powered YouTube and TikTok Monetization Strategies

Artificial intelligence is transforming how content creators on YouTube and TikTok optimize, scale, and monetize their videos. AI-powered tools help automate video creation, enhance audience engagement, and maximize revenue opportunities through data-driven insights. Whether through AI-generated scripts, automated editing, or predictive analytics, leveraging AI allows creators to increase visibility, improve watch time, and drive higher ad revenue, sponsorships, and affiliate sales.

One of the most effective AI-driven monetization strategies is using AI to streamline video production. AI-powered scriptwriting tools like ChatGPT, Jasper, and Copy.ai assist creators in generating compelling video scripts based on trending topics and audience interests. These tools analyze past high-performing content, suggest engaging hooks, and refine messaging to align with platform algorithms. This eliminates writer's block and ensures that videos are structured for maximum engagement. AI also generates video outlines and captions that enhance accessibility and retention.

AI-driven video editing software significantly reduces post-production time while improving content quality. Tools like Runway ML, Magisto, and Adobe Premiere Pro's AI-powered features automate tasks such as cutting, color correction, and scene transitions. AI can also detect the most engaging moments in long-form videos and repurpose them into short clips for TikTok, Instagram Reels, and YouTube Shorts, increasing content reach across multiple platforms. This maximizes monetization potential by diversifying revenue streams from both short-form and long-form video content.

Optimizing video titles, descriptions, and thumbnails is another way AI enhances monetization. AI-powered tools like TubeBuddy, VidIQ, and Morningfame analyze YouTube and TikTok's search algorithms to suggest high-ranking keywords and metadata that improve video discoverability. AI-generated thumbnails analyze past successful designs and recommend the most engaging layouts, colors, and text placements. Since thumbnails and titles are critical for click-through rates, AI optimization increases views and boosts ad revenue.

AI-powered analytics tools help creators refine their monetization strategies by predicting which content types will generate the most revenue. YouTube and TikTok analytics provide insights into audience behavior, watch time, and engagement patterns, but AI-driven tools like Social Blade and Unmetric go further by offering predictive analytics on trending content and competitor performance. By identifying high-converting content formats and ideal posting times, creators can maximize ad impressions and increase sponsorship opportunities.

AI-enhanced voiceovers and avatars are also changing how creators monetize content. Tools like Synthesia and ElevenLabs generate realistic AI-driven voiceovers, allowing creators to produce narration without recording their own voice. This is especially useful for automation-driven channels such as explainer videos, news recaps, and product reviews. AI-generated avatars, such as those offered by Replika and DeepBrain AI, enable faceless content creation, allowing users to build engaging virtual influencers or tutorial-based channels without being on camera. These AI-driven approaches lower production costs while maintaining consistent content output.

AI-driven audience personalization and automated engagement further enhance monetization strategies. AI-powered chatbots and auto-reply systems help manage viewer interactions, respond to comments, and increase community engagement without manual effort. This creates a more interactive experience, boosting viewer loyalty and watch time, which in turn improves revenue from YouTube's Partner Program and TikTok's Creator Fund. AI also enables dynamic ad placement, optimizing the timing and positioning of mid-roll ads to maximize earnings without disrupting viewer experience.

Affiliate marketing and product sales are also benefiting from AI integration. AI-driven recommendation engines analyze user behavior and suggest personalized affiliate products, increasing conversion rates for creators who promote sponsored items. TikTok's AI-driven shopping features help influencers seamlessly integrate product links into their content, turning viral videos into direct sales opportunities. YouTube's AI-powered merch shelf and integrated store links allow creators to sell branded products based on viewer preferences. By using AI to automate product recommendations, creators enhance their revenue potential without additional manual effort.

AI-powered monetization strategies allow YouTube and TikTok creators to work smarter, not harder, by automating repetitive tasks, optimizing content for visibility, and increasing engagement through personalization. Those who embrace AI tools for scriptwriting, editing, analytics, and audience interaction gain a competitive advantage in scaling their platforms and maximizing revenue. As AI continues to evolve, its role in video monetization will only expand, providing more opportunities for creators to generate sustainable income with minimal overhead.

Creating AI-Enhanced Online Courses and Memberships

AI is transforming the way online courses and memberships are created, delivered, and monetized. AI-driven tools help course creators streamline content production, personalize learning experiences, and optimize marketing strategies for maximum student engagement and retention. By leveraging AI, educators, entrepreneurs, and businesses can build scalable online education platforms that provide a more interactive and tailored learning experience while increasing revenue potential.

One of the most powerful applications of AI in online course creation is automated content generation. AI-powered writing tools like ChatGPT, Jasper, and Copy.ai assist in structuring course outlines, generating lesson scripts, and creating high-quality learning materials. AI analyzes industry trends and learner preferences to suggest relevant course topics, ensuring that content aligns with market demand. AI-generated quizzes, assignments, and assessments further enhance the learning experience by providing automated feedback and tracking student progress.

AI-driven video production tools streamline course creation by automating editing, voiceovers, and interactive elements.

Platforms like Synthesia and Pictory allow course creators to generate professional-quality video lectures using AI avatars and voice synthesis, eliminating the need for on-camera recordings. AI-enhanced video editing tools like Runway ML and Adobe Sensei optimize visuals, remove filler content, and generate captions automatically, making course production more efficient and cost-effective.

Personalized learning experiences are another key advantage of AI-enhanced online courses. AI-powered learning management systems (LMS) analyze student engagement and behavior to deliver customized learning paths. Platforms like Teachable and Kajabi integrate AI-driven recommendations to suggest lessons based on individual progress, ensuring that students receive content tailored to their needs. Adaptive learning systems use AI to adjust course difficulty and pacing, allowing students to learn at their own speed while improving knowledge retention.

AI also enhances community engagement within membership platforms by automating interactions and providing personalized support. AI chatbots and virtual assistants help answer student questions, recommend resources, and facilitate discussions within course communities. AI-powered sentiment analysis tools monitor student feedback and engagement, allowing course creators to refine content and improve student satisfaction. By integrating AI-driven discussion forums and peer-to-peer networking, memberships become more interactive, fostering long-term student loyalty.

Marketing and sales automation powered by AI increase course enrollments and membership conversions. AI-driven analytics tools like HubSpot and ConvertKit analyze user behavior to optimize email marketing campaigns, social media ads, and sales funnels. AI-powered A/B testing helps identify the most effective course titles, pricing strategies, and promotional content, ensuring higher conversion rates. AI-generated lead magnets, such as personalized course recommendations and targeted ad copy, attract the right audience and increase enrollment numbers.

AI-powered gamification features enhance student engagement and retention within membership platforms. AI analyzes learner behavior to suggest rewards, progress badges, and achievement milestones that motivate students to complete courses. AI-driven interactive assessments provide instant feedback, encouraging active participation and reinforcing learning outcomes. By incorporating AI-powered engagement strategies, course creators can reduce dropout rates and increase long-term membership value.

The scalability of AI-enhanced online courses allows educators and entrepreneurs to expand their reach without increasing workload. AI automates administrative tasks such as student onboarding, certification issuance, and course updates, freeing up time for creators to focus on delivering high-value content. AI-driven course translation and localization tools enable global accessibility, allowing courses to reach a broader audience across different languages and cultures.

By integrating AI into course creation, engagement, marketing, and automation, educators and entrepreneurs can build profitable online courses and memberships that provide a superior learning experience. AI-powered personalization, automated content generation, and predictive analytics help optimize every stage of the learning journey, ensuring that students remain engaged while maximizing revenue potential. Those who embrace AI-driven strategies in online education will gain a competitive edge in an increasingly digital learning landscape.

Chapter 6: AI-Enhanced Copywriting and Marketing Strategies

Writing High-Converting Ads and Sales Pages with AI

AI is revolutionizing copywriting and marketing by enabling businesses to craft high-converting ads and sales pages with speed, precision, and data-driven insights. AI-powered tools analyze customer behavior, industry trends, and conversion metrics to generate persuasive, results-oriented content that drives engagement and sales. Whether for paid advertisements, landing pages, or email marketing campaigns, AI enhances every aspect of digital marketing by optimizing messaging, improving targeting, and automating content creation.

AI-driven copywriting platforms like Jasper, Copy.ai, and Writesonic generate ad copy tailored to different platforms, audiences, and objectives. These tools analyze successful campaigns to determine the best-performing headlines, calls to action, and persuasive techniques. By leveraging AI-generated content, marketers can quickly test multiple variations of ad copy, optimizing for click-through rates and conversions. AI also ensures that messaging aligns with brand voice, making copywriting more efficient while maintaining consistency across marketing channels.

One of the most significant advantages of AI in ad creation is real-time performance optimization. AI-powered ad platforms like Facebook Ads Manager and Google Ads use machine learning to analyze engagement data and adjust campaigns for maximum effectiveness. AI continuously refines ad copy by testing different headlines, descriptions, and visuals, ensuring that marketing messages remain relevant and impactful. Predictive analytics help marketers identify which ad variations will resonate most with target audiences, eliminating guesswork and improving return on investment.

AI enhances sales pages by structuring persuasive content that leads potential customers through a seamless conversion journey. AI-powered tools analyze psychological triggers, such as urgency, social proof, and scarcity, to craft compelling sales page elements that increase buyer confidence. AI-generated headlines, subheadings, and body copy are optimized for engagement, ensuring that sales pages are clear, persuasive, and action-driven. AI also assists in creating dynamic content that adapts based on user behavior, displaying personalized product recommendations or testimonials to enhance credibility and conversion rates.

Search engine optimization plays a critical role in high-converting sales pages, and AI optimizes copy for maximum search visibility. AI-driven SEO tools like Surfer SEO, Clearscope, and Frase analyze top-ranking content to recommend keyword placement, readability improvements, and content structure enhancements. AI ensures that sales pages rank higher in search results, increasing organic traffic and reducing reliance on paid advertising. By aligning copy with SEO best practices, AI-powered marketing strategies attract more qualified leads, ultimately driving more sales.

Personalization is another area where AI significantly improves ad and sales page effectiveness. AI-driven marketing automation tools like HubSpot and Marketo analyze user data to generate personalized ad campaigns and tailored sales page experiences. AI can dynamically adjust messaging, offers, and pricing based on user demographics, past interactions, and behavioral triggers. This level of personalization enhances customer engagement and increases the likelihood of conversions by delivering content that feels highly relevant to each visitor.

AI also streamlines the A/B testing process, allowing marketers to test different versions of ad copy and sales page elements at scale. AI analyzes engagement metrics such as bounce rates, click-through rates, and conversion rates to determine which variations perform best. By automating testing and refinement, AI ensures that marketers maximize their advertising budget and optimize content for higher sales.

AI-powered chatbots and virtual assistants further enhance sales page effectiveness by providing real-time customer support and answering buyer questions. These AI-driven tools guide potential customers through the purchasing process, addressing objections and reinforcing value propositions. By integrating AI-powered conversational marketing, brands improve user experience and increase conversion rates by offering personalized interactions at every stage of the sales funnel.

By leveraging AI in copywriting and marketing, businesses can create high-converting ads and sales pages that drive revenue with minimal manual effort. AI-powered tools enable faster content creation, data-driven optimization, and personalized marketing strategies that enhance customer engagement. As AI continues to advance, marketers who embrace AI-driven copywriting techniques will gain a competitive edge, maximizing conversions while streamlining their advertising and sales efforts.

Email Marketing Automation and AI-Powered Personalization

AI has transformed email marketing by automating campaign workflows, optimizing content, and delivering highly personalized messages that drive engagement and conversions. Traditional email marketing strategies often require manual effort to segment audiences, craft compelling copy, and analyze campaign performance. AI-powered tools streamline these processes, enabling businesses to send the right message to the right audience at the right time, maximizing open rates, click-through rates, and overall revenue.

AI-driven email automation platforms like Mailchimp, HubSpot, and ActiveCampaign use machine learning to analyze customer behavior, segment audiences, and personalize messaging at scale. These tools track user interactions, such as website visits, purchase history, and email engagement, to automatically trigger emails based on specific actions. This ensures that subscribers receive timely and relevant messages, such as abandoned cart reminders, personalized product recommendations, or follow-up emails after a purchase.

One of the most powerful applications of AI in email marketing is predictive analytics. AI algorithms analyze historical data to predict which types of emails are most likely to resonate with specific audience segments. By understanding user preferences and engagement patterns, AI helps marketers craft subject lines, calls to action, and content formats that increase email open rates and conversions. AI-powered platforms like Phrasee and Persado use natural language processing to generate subject lines and email copy optimized for engagement, ensuring that each message aligns with audience preferences.

Personalization is a key driver of email marketing success, and AI enables deep customization at scale. AI-powered dynamic content generation tailors email messaging based on individual user behavior, demographics, and interests. Instead of sending generic email blasts, AI can generate personalized recommendations, special offers, and curated content that align with each subscriber's preferences. AI-driven tools like Rasa.io use machine learning to curate personalized newsletters based on user reading habits, delivering content that feels relevant and valuable.

AI also optimizes email send times to ensure maximum engagement. AI-powered scheduling tools analyze when individual subscribers are most likely to open and interact with emails, allowing marketers to send messages at the optimal time for each recipient. This eliminates guesswork and improves overall campaign performance. By using AI-driven testing and real-time adjustments, businesses can fine-tune their email strategies to maximize effectiveness.

Automated A/B testing powered by AI further enhances email marketing campaigns by analyzing different versions of subject lines, images, and email layouts to determine which elements perform best. AI continuously tests and refines messaging to improve conversion rates, ensuring that each campaign is optimized based on data-driven insights. AI-powered analytics tools also track user sentiment and engagement trends, allowing businesses to adapt their email marketing strategies based on real-time feedback.

AI-powered chatbots and virtual assistants are also enhancing email marketing automation. AI-driven email assistants can analyze customer inquiries and generate personalized responses, reducing the need for manual email replies. Automated email responses can address frequently asked questions, provide product recommendations, and nurture leads through the sales funnel, improving customer experience and increasing conversions.

By leveraging AI in email marketing automation and personalization, businesses can create highly targeted, data-driven campaigns that drive engagement and revenue. AI-powered tools eliminate the need for manual segmentation, optimize messaging based on predictive analytics, and ensure that emails reach subscribers at the right time with the right content. As AI continues to advance, businesses that embrace AI-driven email marketing strategies will see increased efficiency, stronger customer relationships, and higher conversion rates.

AI in E-Commerce: Optimizing Product Descriptions and Customer Engagement

Artificial intelligence is transforming e-commerce by automating content creation, improving customer interactions, and optimizing marketing strategies. AI-powered tools enhance product descriptions to drive conversions while providing personalized shopping experiences that keep customers engaged. By leveraging AI, online retailers can streamline operations, improve search visibility, and increase sales with minimal manual effort.

AI-generated product descriptions save time and ensure consistency across large inventories. Tools like Jasper, Copy.ai, and ChatGPT analyze product features, specifications, and customer intent to generate compelling descriptions that highlight key selling points. AI ensures that product descriptions are optimized for clarity, readability, and emotional appeal, making them more persuasive to potential buyers. AI also enhances search engine optimization by incorporating high-ranking keywords, improving visibility on marketplaces like Amazon, Shopify, and eBay.

Personalization plays a critical role in customer engagement, and AI enables dynamic content that adapts to individual shoppers. AI-powered recommendation engines analyze browsing history, purchase patterns, and user preferences to suggest relevant products. Platforms like Amazon and Shopify use AI to display personalized recommendations based on previous interactions, increasing the likelihood of conversions. AI-driven dynamic pricing adjusts product prices in real-time based on demand, competitor pricing, and customer behavior, optimizing profitability while maintaining competitiveness.

Chatbots and AI-powered virtual assistants improve customer engagement by providing instant support and personalized shopping guidance. AI chatbots integrated into e-commerce platforms handle inquiries about product details, shipping information, and returns, reducing response times and enhancing customer satisfaction. AI assistants analyze customer questions to provide tailored recommendations, simulate in-store experiences, and even upsell complementary products based on user preferences. Tools like Drift, Intercom, and ManyChat automate customer interactions, ensuring 24/7 support while maintaining a conversational, human-like experience.

AI also enhances customer retention by analyzing sentiment and engagement data. AI-driven sentiment analysis tools evaluate customer feedback, reviews, and social media interactions to identify trends in consumer satisfaction. Businesses use these insights to refine product offerings, improve customer service, and personalize marketing campaigns. AI-powered email automation tools track customer interactions and send targeted promotions, abandoned cart reminders, and re-engagement campaigns based on user behavior.

Visual AI enhances e-commerce experiences by improving image search capabilities and product visualization. AI-driven tools like Google Lens and Pinterest Visual Search allow customers to search for products using images instead of text. AI-powered augmented reality features enable shoppers to visualize products in real-world settings, increasing confidence in purchase decisions. These innovations improve user experience and reduce return rates by providing more accurate product previews.

By integrating AI into e-commerce, businesses can optimize product descriptions, enhance customer engagement, and improve overall sales performance. AI automates content creation, personalizes the shopping journey, and provides data-driven insights that help retailers stay competitive in a rapidly evolving market. As AI technology continues to advance, its role in e-commerce will become even more essential, shaping the future of online retail by delivering smarter, more personalized, and highly efficient shopping experiences.

AI Chatbots and Customer Service Automation

AI chatbots and customer service automation have revolutionized how businesses interact with customers, providing instant, efficient, and personalized support. By leveraging artificial intelligence, companies can reduce response times, handle large volumes of inquiries, and enhance customer satisfaction without requiring a full-time human support team. AI-powered chatbots and automation tools streamline communication, improve user experiences, and optimize customer service operations across industries.

AI chatbots use natural language processing (NLP) to understand and respond to customer queries in a conversational manner. Advanced AI models, such as ChatGPT,

IBM Watson, and Drift, analyze user input, detect intent, and generate relevant responses, making interactions feel more human-like. These chatbots can handle common inquiries, such as order status updates, refund policies, and troubleshooting steps, allowing businesses to provide 24/7 customer support without the need for live agents.

One of the key benefits of AI-powered chatbots is their ability to personalize interactions. AI analyzes customer history, past purchases, and browsing behavior to tailor responses and recommendations. Personalized support increases customer satisfaction by addressing individual needs efficiently. E-commerce platforms use AI chatbots to suggest products based on user preferences, while financial institutions leverage AI to provide personalized account assistance and fraud detection alerts.

AI-driven customer service automation extends beyond chatbots. Automated ticketing systems categorize and prioritize customer issues, ensuring that urgent matters receive immediate attention. AI-powered sentiment analysis detects customer emotions in text-based interactions, allowing businesses to escalate concerns that require human intervention. AI also assists live agents by providing real-time response suggestions and relevant knowledge base articles, reducing resolution times and improving service quality.

Multichannel AI chatbots enhance customer engagement by integrating seamlessly across websites, social media, and messaging apps. Businesses deploy AI chatbots on platforms like Facebook Messenger, WhatsApp, and Instagram to provide instant support and answer inquiries. This omnichannel approach ensures that customers receive consistent assistance regardless of their preferred communication channel, improving brand reliability and trust.

AI chatbots also contribute to sales and lead generation by engaging potential customers through automated conversations. AI-powered assistants qualify leads, collect contact information, and schedule appointments, enabling sales teams to focus on high-value prospects. Chatbots integrated with AI-driven recommendation engines suggest products and promotions based on user behavior, increasing conversion rates and customer retention.

Data collection and analysis play a significant role in AI-driven customer service automation. AI chatbots gather insights from interactions, identifying common pain points, frequently asked questions, and customer preferences. Businesses use this data to refine their support strategies, improve self-service options, and enhance product offerings. AI-powered predictive analytics help businesses anticipate customer needs, proactively offering solutions before issues arise.

As AI technology continues to evolve, chatbots and automation tools will become even more sophisticated, offering more natural, context-aware conversations and improved problem-solving capabilities. Businesses that implement AI-driven customer service automation gain a competitive advantage by providing faster, more efficient, and highly personalized support experiences. By reducing operational costs while enhancing customer satisfaction, AI chatbots and automation are reshaping the future of customer service across industries.

Chapter 7: Ethical AI Use – Avoiding Plagiarism, Bias, and Low-Quality Output

The Ethics of AI-Generated Content: Where to Draw the Line

As AI-generated content becomes increasingly prevalent in writing, marketing, and creative industries, ethical concerns regarding originality, bias, and quality must be addressed. While AI is a powerful tool that enhances productivity and efficiency, it also raises questions about authorship, credibility, and the potential misuse of generated content. Understanding where to draw the line between responsible AI use and ethical pitfalls is crucial for businesses, content creators, and digital marketers who rely on AI for content generation.

One of the primary ethical concerns surrounding AI-generated content is plagiarism. AI models are trained on vast datasets, which include publicly available information, books, articles, and online content. When AI generates text, there is a risk that it may replicate existing content without proper attribution. While AI does not intentionally copy material, there have been cases where generated text closely resembles original sources. To avoid plagiarism, content creators must fact-check and refine AI-generated text, ensuring it is unique and original. AI detection tools, such as Turnitin and Copyscape, can help verify authenticity and prevent unintentional duplication. Responsible AI users should treat AI as an assistant rather than a replacement for human creativity, using it to generate ideas rather than merely reformat existing content.

Bias in AI-generated content is another major ethical challenge. AI models learn from the data they are trained on, which means they can inadvertently reflect biases present in that data. Whether in gender representation, racial stereotypes, or political perspectives, AI-generated content can perpetuate unintended biases that distort objectivity. This is especially concerning in journalism, legal writing, and content related to sensitive social issues. Ethical AI use requires content creators to review outputs critically, applying human judgment to identify and correct biases before publishing content. AI should be seen as a tool for assistance rather than a definitive source of truth. Companies developing AI models must also work to diversify training data and implement bias mitigation techniques to ensure fair and balanced outputs.

Quality control is another crucial aspect of ethical AI use. While AI can generate large volumes of content quickly, quality is not always guaranteed. AI-generated text can sometimes be vague, repetitive, or lack coherence. Over-reliance on AI for content creation can result in generic or misleading information that does not meet professional or journalistic standards. Businesses and marketers must maintain editorial oversight to refine AI-generated text, ensuring it aligns with brand messaging, industry expertise, and audience expectations. Quality AI-driven content should blend human insight with AI-generated efficiency, striking a balance between automation and authenticity.

Transparency in AI-generated content is also an important ethical consideration. Readers, consumers, and clients should be informed when content is created or heavily influenced by AI. Companies using AI-generated marketing copy, social media posts, or customer support responses should disclose AI involvement to maintain trust and accountability. Search engines and social media platforms are beginning to implement policies that require transparency in AI-generated content, making it necessary for businesses to comply with evolving guidelines. Ethical AI use includes openly acknowledging AI's role in content creation while ensuring that final outputs maintain human oversight and credibility.

AI's role in ethical content creation is not about eliminating its use but about setting responsible guidelines that ensure integrity, originality, and fairness. Content creators and businesses that embrace AI while maintaining ethical standards will gain a competitive advantage, fostering trust among their audiences and delivering high-quality content that aligns with industry best practices. The future of AI in content creation depends on responsible use, where technology enhances human creativity rather than replacing it. By drawing clear ethical lines, businesses and creators can harness AI's power while maintaining authenticity, accountability, and trustworthiness in an AI-driven world.

Overcoming AI Bias and Ensuring Authenticity

AI bias is a growing concern in content creation, decision-making, and automated systems. Because AI learns from existing data, it can unintentionally reinforce stereotypes, favor certain perspectives, or generate misleading information. Ensuring authenticity and fairness in AI-generated content requires proactive measures, including refining training data, applying human oversight, and implementing ethical guidelines. By addressing bias and maintaining authenticity, businesses, content creators, and marketers can use AI responsibly while preserving credibility and trust.

One of the main causes of AI bias is the data it is trained on. AI models, such as those used for writing, image generation, and predictive analytics, rely on large datasets sourced from books, websites, and digital archives. If these datasets contain biased language, cultural stereotypes, or historical inaccuracies, the AI may replicate and amplify those biases in its outputs. To overcome this, developers and content creators must ensure diverse and balanced training data. AI training should include perspectives from different cultures, genders, and socio-economic backgrounds to create more inclusive and unbiased content. Companies investing in AI should prioritize ethical data collection and transparency in model training.

Human oversight plays a critical role in reducing AI bias. AI-generated content should never be published or used without human review to verify accuracy, fairness, and context. Editors, fact-checkers, and industry experts should assess AI-generated material to ensure it aligns with ethical standards. This is especially important in fields like journalism, legal writing, and healthcare, where misinformation or biased narratives can have serious consequences. Implementing a hybrid approach—where AI assists in content creation while humans refine and approve final outputs—ensures higher authenticity and reliability.

Ensuring authenticity in AI-generated content also requires transparency. Readers, consumers, and audiences should know when AI has played a role in generating content. Disclosing AI involvement fosters trust and helps prevent the spread of misinformation. Businesses using AI for customer support, marketing, or content creation should clearly communicate how AI contributes to the final product. Some organizations are adopting AI watermarks or labels to distinguish AI-generated content from human-created material, reinforcing authenticity while maintaining accountability.

Another effective way to overcome AI bias is to implement ethical AI frameworks that guide content creation and decision-making. These frameworks include regular audits of AI outputs, bias detection tools, and continuous learning models that adapt to new, unbiased data. AI-powered sentiment analysis can also help detect unintended bias in text, ensuring that messaging remains neutral, inclusive, and aligned with brand values. Companies committed to responsible AI use should prioritize ethical guidelines that promote fairness, inclusivity, and objectivity.

User feedback and community engagement further help identify and correct AI bias. Allowing audiences to report inaccuracies, flag biased content, or suggest improvements enables continuous refinement of AI-generated outputs. AI-driven platforms can integrate user feedback loops to improve content quality and responsiveness over time. By actively listening to users and incorporating their insights, businesses and creators can ensure that AI-generated content remains relevant, unbiased, and aligned with audience expectations.

While AI bias is a complex challenge, it can be managed through ethical AI development, human oversight, transparency, and user feedback. Organizations that take proactive steps to mitigate bias and ensure authenticity will build trust, improve content credibility, and create fairer digital experiences. AI should be a tool for empowerment, helping businesses and creators enhance productivity without compromising integrity or inclusivity. By implementing responsible AI practices, content creators can harness the benefits of AI while ensuring that their work reflects diverse, accurate, and authentic perspectives.

AI vs. Human Creativity: Striking the Perfect Balance

The rise of AI-generated content has sparked an ongoing debate about its impact on human creativity. While AI can generate text, images, music, and even video with remarkable speed and efficiency, it lacks the depth of human experience, intuition, and emotional intelligence that define truly original and meaningful creations. Striking the perfect balance between AI and human creativity is essential for leveraging the strengths of both while maintaining authenticity, originality, and ethical integrity in content creation.

AI excels at automating repetitive tasks, analyzing data, and optimizing content for engagement. AI-driven tools can generate blog posts, marketing copy, product descriptions, and even entire books within seconds, providing businesses and creators with scalable content solutions. AI also enhances creativity by offering instant brainstorming assistance, suggesting unique angles, and generating outlines that help writers and designers develop fresh ideas faster. By handling time-consuming aspects of content creation, AI frees up human creators to focus on higher-level strategy, refinement, and storytelling.

However, AI lacks personal experiences, emotions, and cultural context, which are fundamental elements of human creativity. While AI can mimic language patterns and artistic styles, it does not possess an intrinsic understanding of human emotions, history, or personal expression. Creativity is often driven by lived experiences, intuition, and an ability to connect with audiences on an emotional level—something AI cannot replicate authentically. Human creators bring originality, perspective, and artistic intention that AI alone cannot produce.

The ideal approach is a hybrid model where AI acts as a tool to support and enhance human creativity rather than replace it. Writers can use AI-generated drafts as a starting point but refine them with their unique voice and insights. Designers can use AI-assisted tools to automate layout generation or enhance visual effects while infusing their work with originality. Musicians can use AI-generated compositions for inspiration but adjust melodies, lyrics, and rhythms to reflect their artistic vision. By integrating AI into the creative process without relying on it entirely, creators maintain authenticity while benefiting from AI's efficiency.

Striking this balance also involves ethical considerations. Over-reliance on AI-generated content can lead to a decline in originality and a saturation of generic, formulaic material. Businesses and content creators must ensure that AI is used responsibly, with human oversight to maintain quality and integrity. Transparency in AI-generated work helps build trust, ensuring that audiences know when AI has been used in content creation. Setting clear ethical guidelines for AI usage ensures that automation enhances rather than dilutes creative expression.

Collaboration between AI and human creativity represents the future of content creation. AI can process vast amounts of information, generate data-driven insights, and suggest creative possibilities, while humans bring storytelling, emotion, and deeper meaning. The best results come from a thoughtful integration of AI's computational power with human intuition and artistic depth. Those who learn to harness AI as a creative partner rather than a replacement will gain a competitive edge, producing innovative, high-quality content that resonates with audiences while maximizing efficiency and impact.

Case Studies: The Consequences of Unethical AI Use

As AI continues to shape industries, its misuse has led to serious ethical challenges, affecting businesses, individuals, and society as a whole. When AI is deployed without proper oversight, it can result in misinformation, bias, copyright violations, and privacy breaches. Examining real-world cases of unethical AI use highlights the risks involved and the importance of responsible AI implementation.

One of the most high-profile cases of unethical AI use involved deepfake technology. In 2019, manipulated AI-generated videos surfaced featuring political leaders making false statements. These deepfakes spread misinformation, raising concerns about their potential to influence elections, incite public unrest, and undermine trust in media. The incident demonstrated how AI, when used irresponsibly, can blur the line between reality and fiction, leading to widespread misinformation with severe consequences.

Another case involved AI bias in hiring algorithms. A major tech company developed an AI-powered recruitment tool that analyzed resumes and recommended candidates based on past hiring trends. However, the system was found to be biased against women, as it had been trained on historical hiring data that favored male candidates. The algorithm penalized resumes containing words associated with women's activities, leading to discriminatory hiring practices. This case highlighted the dangers of relying on AI without addressing underlying biases in training data, reinforcing the need for human oversight in AI-driven decision-making.

In the financial sector, unethical AI use led to discriminatory lending practices. AI-powered credit scoring models used by banks and lending institutions were found to disproportionately deny loans to minority applicants. The AI models, trained on historical financial data, inherited biases that disadvantaged certain demographics. Regulators stepped in to address the issue, emphasizing the need for transparency in AI decision-making to prevent discrimination and ensure fair access to financial resources.

Copyright infringement is another major ethical issue in AI-generated content. AI models trained on copyrighted material without proper authorization have resulted in legal disputes. A well-known case involved AI-generated artwork that closely resembled existing works by human artists, leading to accusations of plagiarism and intellectual property theft. Some artists found their styles replicated without consent, raising concerns about whether AI-generated creations should be considered original or derivative works. The controversy reinforced the importance of ethical AI training practices and fair compensation for original creators.

Privacy violations have also emerged as a consequence of unethical AI use. AI-powered facial recognition technology has been deployed without user consent, leading to mass surveillance concerns. Several governments and corporations faced backlash for using AI to track individuals without proper data protection policies. The misuse of facial recognition in public spaces and law enforcement raised ethical questions about personal privacy, leading to legal challenges and bans on certain AI-driven surveillance programs.

These case studies demonstrate the far-reaching consequences of unethical AI use. Misinformation, bias, copyright violations, and privacy breaches undermine trust in AI and create risks for businesses and individuals. The solution lies in responsible AI development, transparent decision-making processes, and continuous human oversight. Companies and policymakers must establish ethical guidelines to ensure that AI is used to enhance society rather than harm it. As AI technology advances, maintaining ethical integrity will be crucial in preventing future misuse and building trust in artificial intelligence.

Chapter 8: The AI Creator's Toolkit – The Best AI Tools for Every Need

Breakdown of the Best AI Writing Tools (ChatGPT, Jasper, Copy.ai, etc.)

AI-powered writing tools have revolutionized content creation by offering efficiency, scalability, and optimization. Whether for blogs, marketing copy, scripts, or SEO-driven content, AI writing platforms help creators produce high-quality material faster while maintaining consistency and engagement. With various AI-driven tools available, choosing the right one depends on specific needs such as long-form writing, copy generation, or content personalization. Here's a breakdown of some of the best AI writing tools and their key features.

ChatGPT

Developed by OpenAI, ChatGPT is one of the most versatile AI writing assistants. It excels at generating human-like text for a wide range of applications, including blogs, social media captions, scripts, and customer support responses. ChatGPT is ideal for brainstorming, summarizing information, and refining ideas. Its conversational style allows for interactive content creation, making it useful for storytelling, dialogue writing, and audience engagement. While it provides valuable insights, human oversight is necessary to ensure factual accuracy and originality.

Jasper

Jasper is one of the most advanced AI tools for marketing and sales-driven content. It offers specialized templates for ad copy, product descriptions, email marketing, and long-form articles. Jasper's ability to maintain brand voice and style makes it an excellent choice for businesses looking to automate content while keeping it personalized. It integrates well with SEO tools, making it a strong option for search-optimized blog writing. Jasper's Boss Mode allows users to give direct commands, making it more efficient for structured content creation.

Copy.ai

Designed primarily for marketers, Copy.ai specializes in generating short-form copy for ads, social media, and email campaigns. It offers pre-built templates for persuasive headlines, engaging social posts, and product descriptions. Copy.ai is best suited for businesses that require high-volume content generation without compromising on quality. While it excels in quick, impactful messaging, it is less effective for in-depth long-form writing compared to tools like Jasper and ChatGPT.

Writesonic

Writesonic is an AI-powered writing tool known for its diverse range of features, including article writing, ad copy generation, and paraphrasing. It offers both short-form and long-form content options, making it a versatile choice for marketers and bloggers. Writesonic's AI editor allows users to refine generated text, ensuring that the final output aligns with brand voice and industry standards. It also includes an AI-driven chatbot for customer service and content automation.

Rytr

Rytr is an affordable AI writing assistant that caters to small businesses and individual creators. It provides content templates for various industries, including e-commerce, real estate, and technology. Rytr's strength lies in its ability to generate cost-effective content quickly. While it may not have the same advanced customization features as Jasper or Copy.ai, it remains a solid option for startups looking for budget-friendly AI writing solutions.

Writesonic vs. Jasper vs. ChatGPT: Which One to Choose?

Choosing the right AI writing tool depends on specific needs. ChatGPT is best for interactive, conversational, and research-driven writing. Jasper is ideal for marketing, sales, and SEO-optimized long-form content. Copy.ai excels at quick, persuasive ad copy and social media content. Writesonic provides an all-in-one solution for businesses seeking affordability with diverse writing capabilities.

Best Practices for Using AI Writing Tools

To maximize the effectiveness of AI-generated content, creators should provide clear and detailed prompts, refine AI-generated drafts with human oversight, and combine AI efficiency with creative storytelling. AI should be used as a tool for enhancement rather than a replacement for originality.

As AI continues to evolve, the tools available for content creation will become even more powerful. By leveraging the right AI writing platforms, businesses and content creators can streamline workflows, improve engagement, and maintain a competitive edge in digital marketing and content production.

AI Tools for Image & Video Creation (Runway, MidJourney, DALL·E)

Artificial intelligence has transformed the way creators generate visual content, making high-quality images and videos more accessible than ever. AI-powered tools like Runway, MidJourney, and DALL·E allow artists, marketers, and content creators to produce stunning visuals without requiring advanced design or video editing skills. These tools streamline the creative process by automating image generation, enhancing video production, and enabling new forms of artistic expression.

Runway – AI for Video Editing and Effects

Runway is one of the most advanced AI-powered video creation tools, offering a suite of features that simplify editing, animation, and special effects. It allows users to remove backgrounds, enhance footage, and apply cinematic effects with minimal effort. One of Runway's standout features is AI-powered rotoscoping, which enables seamless object isolation without frame-by-frame manual work. Additionally, its AI-driven text-to-video capabilities allow creators to generate video clips from text prompts, making it a valuable tool for social media content, advertising, and film production.

MidJourney – AI-Generated Artistic Imagery

MidJourney is an AI-driven image generation tool that produces highly detailed and artistic visuals based on text prompts. Unlike traditional design software, MidJourney creates stunning digital paintings, concept art, and surreal illustrations in various styles, from hyper-realistic to abstract. It has gained popularity among artists, designers, and marketers looking to generate unique, high-quality visuals for branding, digital storytelling, and creative projects. Its ability to interpret prompts creatively makes it an excellent tool for producing visually compelling content for social media, book covers, and digital marketing campaigns.

DALL·E – AI Image Generation with Realism and Precision

DALL·E, developed by OpenAI, is a powerful AI image generator capable of creating photorealistic visuals from text descriptions. It excels at producing detailed compositions, making it a valuable tool for product mockups, advertising, and content marketing. DALL·E can generate unique visuals tailored to specific needs, eliminating reliance on stock images. It also supports image editing, allowing users to modify existing images by adding or replacing elements using AI-driven tools.

How AI Image and Video Tools Are Changing Content Creation

AI-powered visual tools are reshaping content creation by automating design and video production. Marketers use AI-generated images for ad campaigns, social media posts, and website visuals, while filmmakers and content creators rely on AI-assisted video editing to streamline production workflows. These tools save time, reduce costs, and provide creative flexibility by enabling users to generate high-quality content without extensive technical skills.

Choosing the Right AI Tool for Your Needs

The best AI tool depends on the type of content required. Runway is ideal for video editing, visual effects, and AI-driven animation. MidJourney is best for digital artwork and concept imagery, offering highly stylized visuals. DALL·E is perfect for realistic image generation, particularly for commercial use and product visualization.

AI-powered image and video creation tools provide endless possibilities for designers, marketers, and content creators. By integrating AI into their workflow, creators can enhance efficiency, produce professional-quality visuals, and unlock new creative opportunities in digital content production. As AI technology continues to evolve, these tools will become even more sophisticated, further revolutionizing the way visual content is generated and consumed.

AI in Music and Voice Synthesis (AIVA, ElevenLabs, Murf)

Artificial intelligence is transforming the way music and voice content are created, making high-quality compositions and realistic voiceovers more accessible than ever. AI-driven tools like AIVA, ElevenLabs, and Murf enable musicians, content creators, and businesses to generate professional-grade audio with minimal effort. These technologies streamline production, enhance creativity, and open new possibilities for personalized and automated sound design.

AIVA – AI-Generated Music Composition

AIVA (Artificial Intelligence Virtual Artist) is one of the most advanced AI music composition tools, designed to create original scores for various applications, including film, video games, and advertising. AIVA analyzes classical and contemporary compositions to generate melodies, harmonies, and arrangements that sound human-like. Users can customize music styles, structure, and instrumentation, making it a valuable tool for composers and content creators looking to produce royalty-free music. AIVA is particularly useful for independent filmmakers, game developers, and marketers who need high-quality background music without expensive licensing fees.

ElevenLabs – AI-Powered Voice Cloning and Narration

ElevenLabs specializes in AI voice synthesis, offering hyper-realistic voice cloning and text-to-speech generation. This tool enables users to create lifelike voiceovers for audiobooks, podcasts, videos, and virtual assistants. Unlike traditional robotic-sounding text-to-speech software, ElevenLabs produces natural intonations, accents, and emotions, making AI-generated speech almost indistinguishable from human voices. Content creators can use ElevenLabs to produce high-quality narrations in multiple languages, allowing for greater accessibility and localization. It is particularly useful for audiobook production, video storytelling, and automated customer support voiceovers.

Murf – AI Voiceovers for Business and Content Creation

Murf is a versatile AI-powered voice synthesis tool that provides realistic voiceovers for presentations, training videos, e-learning content, and advertisements. It offers a wide range of voices, accents, and tones, allowing users to customize voiceovers to fit their specific needs. Murf's AI-driven text-to-speech engine ensures smooth, natural-sounding narration, eliminating the need for professional voice actors. Businesses and educators use Murf to create engaging audio content efficiently, making it an ideal solution for explainer videos, corporate training, and multimedia projects.

The Impact of AI in Music and Voice Synthesis

AI-generated music and voice synthesis tools are reshaping the creative landscape by making professional audio production more accessible and cost-effective. Musicians can use AI-generated compositions as inspiration or backing tracks, while businesses can automate high-quality voiceovers for marketing and customer engagement. AI-powered voice synthesis also enhances accessibility by providing multilingual support and adaptive voice features for people with disabilities.

Choosing the Right AI Tool for Your Needs

The best AI tool depends on the type of audio content required. AIVA is ideal for music composition and orchestration, ElevenLabs excels at hyper-realistic voice cloning and audiobook narration, while Murf provides high-quality voiceovers for business and educational content.

AI in music and voice synthesis is unlocking new creative possibilities, enabling users to produce high-quality soundscapes and voiceovers effortlessly. As these technologies continue to evolve, AI-generated audio will become an integral part of media production, enhancing storytelling, marketing, and digital experiences across industries.

Comparing Free vs. Paid AI Tools: What's Worth the Investment?

AI tools have revolutionized content creation, marketing, and automation, but not all tools offer the same level of functionality. Free AI tools provide accessible solutions for beginners and small-scale users, while paid tools offer advanced features, better customization, and superior output quality. Understanding the differences between free and paid AI tools helps determine when investing in premium versions is worthwhile.

Free AI Tools: Accessibility with Limitations

Free AI tools provide a great starting point for those new to AI-driven content creation. Platforms like ChatGPT (free version), Canva (basic plan), and DeepL offer valuable capabilities, such as text generation, image editing, and translation, without requiring financial investment. These tools are ideal for users with limited needs, such as small businesses, students, or freelancers working on occasional projects. However, free AI tools often come with restrictions, such as word limits, limited template access, watermarked outputs, or lower-quality AI processing. Many free tools also have usage caps, requiring users to upgrade for extended access or faster processing speeds.

Paid AI Tools: Advanced Features and Scalability

Paid AI tools offer enhanced performance, greater customization, and access to premium features that significantly improve workflow efficiency. Platforms like Jasper, Copy.ai, and MidJourney provide high-quality content generation with more refined outputs and AI models trained for specific use cases. Paid tools often include integrations with other software, priority customer support, and expanded storage or processing capabilities. Businesses and professionals benefit from premium AI tools when they require bulk content production, advanced analytics, or automation that saves time and boosts productivity.

When to Invest in Paid AI Tools

Investing in paid AI tools is worthwhile for businesses, marketers, and content creators who rely on AI for consistent production. If the free version limits efficiency, affects quality, or restricts access to necessary features, upgrading to a paid plan ensures uninterrupted workflow and better results. Paid AI tools are also essential for users who need high-quality, watermark-free images, SEO-optimized content, AI-generated video editing, or detailed analytics for audience engagement. Additionally, professionals who work with AI for commercial purposes, such as e-commerce product descriptions, ad copy, and branding, gain significant advantages from premium plans that offer more customization and efficiency.

Finding the Right Balance

The decision between free and paid AI tools depends on individual needs. For occasional users, free AI tools may be sufficient, but for those looking to scale operations or enhance content quality, paid versions provide long-term value. Businesses and creators should assess whether the time saved, improved accuracy, and higher output quality justify the cost of a premium subscription. By selecting AI tools strategically, users can maximize their investment and leverage AI to streamline tasks, improve creativity, and enhance digital presence effectively.

Chapter 9: Building an AI-Powered Brand: Standing Out in a Saturated Market

Creating a Unique AI-Driven Personal Brand

In a digital landscape filled with endless content and competition, building a unique personal brand is essential for standing out. AI-powered tools provide a competitive edge by enhancing branding strategies, automating content creation, and personalizing audience engagement. Whether you're an entrepreneur, influencer, or business professional, leveraging AI strategically can help you develop a distinct identity while maintaining authenticity and consistency.

A strong AI-driven personal brand starts with clear positioning. AI analytics tools like Brandwatch and Sprout Social help identify industry trends, audience preferences, and competitive gaps, enabling you to define a unique niche. AI-powered sentiment analysis tools assess online conversations to understand how your brand is perceived, helping refine messaging to align with audience expectations. By using AI for data-driven insights, you can position yourself as an authority in your field with content that resonates.

Content creation is one of the most impactful ways to build a personal brand, and AI enhances this process by generating high-quality material efficiently. AI writing tools like Jasper and Copy.ai assist in crafting blog posts, newsletters, and social media updates that align with your brand voice. AI video editing software such as Runway and Pictory helps create professional video content, ensuring consistency across platforms. AI-generated graphics from tools like MidJourney and Canva ensure visually appealing branding elements, from logos to marketing materials. These AI-driven solutions allow you to maintain a high-volume content strategy without compromising quality.

Authenticity remains a key component of a successful personal brand, even when using AI. AI personalization tools like ChatGPT for chatbots and dynamic email marketing software ensure interactions feel genuine by tailoring responses based on user behavior. AI-driven personalization in newsletters and website experiences enhances audience engagement by delivering relevant recommendations and messaging. However, it is important to balance automation with a human touch, ensuring your brand retains a personal connection with followers.

AI-driven social media strategies amplify brand visibility and engagement. AI-powered scheduling tools such as Hootsuite and Buffer analyze audience behavior to determine the best times to post, while AI recommendation engines suggest trending topics and hashtags. AI chatbots improve interaction by responding to inquiries in real time, fostering a strong connection with your audience. By automating social media engagement intelligently, you can focus on high-impact interactions that strengthen your brand presence.

AI-powered branding also extends to audience analytics and growth strategies. AI tools like SEMrush and Google Analytics track performance metrics, highlighting content that drives engagement and conversions. AI-driven A/B testing tools refine branding strategies by optimizing headlines, color schemes, and messaging elements that resonate most with audiences. By leveraging AI for ongoing optimization, you ensure that your personal brand remains relevant and adaptive to changing market trends.

Standing out in a saturated market requires a combination of AI-driven efficiency and authentic brand storytelling. AI provides the tools to streamline content creation, enhance personalization, and optimize marketing strategies, but true differentiation comes from how you integrate AI with your unique voice, values, and expertise. By using AI as an enabler rather than a replacement for creativity, you can build a strong, memorable personal brand that attracts and retains a loyal audience.

AI in Website and Landing Page Design

Artificial intelligence is transforming website and landing page design by automating development, optimizing user experience, and personalizing content for visitors. AI-powered tools enable businesses, marketers, and entrepreneurs to create high-converting, visually appealing sites without requiring advanced coding or design skills. From AI-generated layouts to automated A/B testing, AI-driven website design enhances efficiency while ensuring professional-quality results.

AI-powered website builders like Wix ADI, Framer, and Bookmark use machine learning to generate fully functional websites based on user input. These platforms analyze industry trends, user preferences, and best design practices to create responsive layouts, choose color schemes, and arrange elements for optimal usability. Instead of manually designing a site from scratch, users can provide a few details about their business, and AI will generate a customized website that aligns with their branding.

Landing pages are critical for capturing leads and driving conversions, and AI helps optimize them for maximum impact. AI-driven platforms like Unbounce and Instapage analyze visitor behavior to personalize landing page content dynamically. AI can adjust headlines, calls to action, and images in real time based on user demographics, location, or browsing history. By tailoring content to individual visitors, AI increases engagement and improves conversion rates.

AI also enhances website copywriting through natural language generation tools like Jasper and Copy.ai. These AI platforms generate compelling headlines, persuasive product descriptions, and SEO-optimized content that improves search engine rankings. AI-powered chatbots further enhance landing pages by providing real-time assistance, answering customer questions, and guiding users through the purchasing process.

AI-driven heatmaps and analytics tools, such as Hotjar and Crazy Egg, track user interactions and identify areas of improvement on websites and landing pages. These tools analyze where users click, scroll, or drop off, allowing businesses to refine layouts, adjust button placements, and improve navigation flow. AI-powered A/B testing automates the process of comparing different page elements, identifying which designs and messages drive the highest conversions.

Personalization is another major advantage of AI in web design. AI tools analyze visitor data to create customized experiences, such as displaying personalized product recommendations, dynamic pricing, and tailored content suggestions. E-commerce platforms like Shopify and WooCommerce integrate AI-driven personalization to enhance customer journeys and increase sales. AI-powered website assistants can also generate individualized content for returning visitors, creating a more engaging and user-centric experience.

AI is making website and landing page design more accessible, efficient, and results-driven. By automating layout generation, optimizing content, and personalizing user interactions, AI helps businesses build high-performing digital experiences that attract and retain visitors. As AI technology continues to evolve, its role in website development will expand, offering even more powerful tools for creating visually stunning, conversion-focused websites without the need for extensive technical expertise.

Building a Loyal Community Around AI-Generated Content

Creating AI-generated content is just the first step; the real challenge lies in building a loyal and engaged community around it. AI-powered content can attract audiences, but genuine connections, trust, and consistent engagement are essential for long-term growth. A successful community is built through personalization, interaction, and value-driven content that resonates with its audience while maintaining authenticity.

Personalization is key to fostering community engagement. AI tools analyze user behavior, preferences, and interactions to deliver tailored content experiences. Platforms like ChatGPT, Jasper, and Copy.ai help create AI-driven blog posts, newsletters, and social media updates that align with audience interests. AI-powered recommendation engines suggest relevant content based on previous engagement, ensuring users receive information that matches their needs and preferences. By delivering personalized AI-generated content, brands and creators strengthen their relationship with their community.

Authenticity plays a crucial role in maintaining trust. While AI enhances efficiency, human oversight is necessary to ensure content retains a personal touch. AI-generated content should be refined to reflect the brand's voice, values, and messaging, making it feel relatable and engaging. Transparency about AI's role in content creation also builds credibility, helping audiences understand the balance between automation and human creativity. Creators who combine AI-driven insights with personal experiences foster deeper connections and loyalty within their community.

Engagement and interaction drive community growth. AI-powered chatbots and virtual assistants enhance communication by responding to inquiries, guiding discussions, and facilitating real-time interactions. Social media AI tools analyze trending conversations and suggest responses that keep audiences engaged. Live Q&A sessions, interactive polls, and community forums encourage participation and help maintain an active and dynamic audience. AI-generated content should not be a one-way broadcast but a conversation that invites discussion, feedback, and user contributions.

Consistent value delivery strengthens loyalty. AI tools help automate content scheduling, ensuring a steady flow of high-quality information. AI-driven analytics tools, such as Google Analytics and Sprout Social, track engagement metrics and audience behavior to refine content strategies. By continuously optimizing AI-generated content based on data insights, creators can ensure their community receives relevant and valuable information, increasing retention and loyalty.

User-generated content and community contributions further enhance engagement. Encouraging followers to share their insights, experiences, and creative work fosters a sense of ownership and belonging. AI-driven content curation tools can highlight user contributions, feature testimonials, and amplify community-generated discussions. By involving the audience in content creation, brands and creators create a collaborative environment that strengthens community bonds.

Building a loyal community around AI-generated content requires a balance between automation and human connection. AI streamlines content creation and personalization, but genuine engagement, transparency, and interactive experiences are what foster lasting relationships. By leveraging AI as a tool while maintaining authenticity and responsiveness, creators can develop a thriving, engaged community that values and trusts their content.

The Future of AI Branding and Personalization

AI is reshaping branding and personalization, allowing businesses to create hyper-targeted experiences that adapt to individual preferences in real time. As AI technology continues to evolve, brands that leverage intelligent automation, data-driven insights, and personalized interactions will gain a competitive advantage in an increasingly digital marketplace. The future of AI-driven branding lies in its ability to enhance customer engagement, refine messaging, and deliver seamless, customized experiences at scale.

AI-powered branding will become more intuitive and dynamic, with machine learning models analyzing vast amounts of consumer data to predict behaviors and preferences. AI tools like Adobe Sensei and HubSpot use predictive analytics to tailor marketing campaigns, ensuring that brand messaging resonates with specific audience segments. As AI systems improve, personalization will go beyond traditional demographics, focusing on individual emotions, habits, and real-time interactions to create content that feels uniquely relevant to each user.

Personalized AI-driven marketing will extend across multiple channels, seamlessly integrating social media, websites, email campaigns, and even offline interactions. AI chatbots and virtual assistants, powered by tools like Drift and ManyChat, will provide customized recommendations, answer queries, and guide customers through the buyer journey in a way that feels natural and conversational. These AI systems will learn from previous interactions, refining their responses to create a more human-like and emotionally intelligent brand experience.

Voice and visual AI will play a crucial role in the future of branding. AI-powered voice assistants such as ElevenLabs and Murf will allow brands to develop distinctive, lifelike voices for their messaging, ensuring a consistent tone across audio and video content. AI-generated images, logos, and video content created with tools like DALL·E and Runway will enable brands to produce dynamic visuals that evolve based on audience engagement and industry trends.

AI branding will also become more interactive and immersive. Augmented reality (AR) and AI-generated virtual environments will create personalized shopping and brand experiences, where customers can explore products, receive tailored recommendations, and engage with digital brand ambassadors. AI-driven personalization engines will adapt product offerings and marketing messages in real time, enhancing engagement and customer satisfaction.

Ethical considerations will be essential in AI-driven branding. As AI personalizes content at an unprecedented level, maintaining transparency and ethical AI practices will be critical to building trust. Consumers will expect brands to use AI responsibly, ensuring data privacy, avoiding manipulation, and maintaining authenticity in AI-generated messaging. Companies that strike a balance between AI-driven efficiency and ethical branding will establish stronger, long-term customer relationships.

The future of AI branding and personalization lies in creating highly adaptive, data-driven, and emotionally intelligent brand experiences. Businesses that embrace AI to deliver meaningful, customized interactions will not only stand out in a crowded marketplace but also foster deeper connections with their audiences. By integrating AI strategically while maintaining human creativity and ethical responsibility, brands will redefine personalization and set new standards for customer engagement.

Chapter 10: Scaling Your AI Business – Automate, Optimize, and Grow

How to Use AI to Automate Business Processes

AI is transforming business operations by automating repetitive tasks, streamlining workflows, and optimizing decision-making. Businesses that integrate AI-powered automation gain efficiency, reduce costs, and free up valuable resources for strategic growth. From customer service and marketing to data analysis and supply chain management, AI-driven automation enables companies to scale operations without sacrificing quality or performance.

One of the most impactful ways to use AI for automation is in customer service. AI-powered chatbots like Drift, Intercom, and ManyChat handle inquiries, provide real-time support, and resolve common customer issues without human intervention. These virtual assistants improve response times, reduce customer service costs, and enhance user experience by offering 24/7 support. AI-driven sentiment analysis tools also track customer feedback, allowing businesses to proactively address concerns and improve service quality.

Marketing automation powered by AI streamlines content creation, social media management, and campaign optimization. AI tools like Jasper and Copy.ai generate high-converting copy for email campaigns, ads, and blog posts, reducing the time spent on content production. Platforms like Hootsuite and Sprout Social use AI to schedule and optimize social media posts, ensuring they reach the right audience at the best time. AI-driven email marketing software, such as HubSpot and Mailchimp, personalizes outreach, segments audiences, and automates follow-up sequences to maximize engagement and conversions.

AI-driven analytics and data processing automate decision-making by extracting insights from vast amounts of information. Predictive analytics tools like Tableau, Google Analytics, and IBM Watson analyze trends, forecast demand, and identify business opportunities. AI-powered CRM systems automate lead scoring and customer segmentation, helping sales teams focus on high-value prospects. Businesses that leverage AI-driven analytics optimize pricing strategies, product recommendations, and sales processes, leading to increased revenue and customer satisfaction.

AI also improves operational efficiency in supply chain and inventory management. AI-driven demand forecasting tools predict stock levels based on market trends, historical data, and seasonal fluctuations. Platforms like ClearMetal and Llamasoft use AI to optimize logistics, reduce waste, and enhance supply chain visibility. Automated inventory tracking minimizes human errors and ensures businesses maintain optimal stock levels, reducing costs and improving fulfillment speed.

HR and recruitment automation is another area where AI is making a significant impact. AI-driven hiring platforms like HireVue and Pymetrics analyze resumes, conduct virtual interviews, and assess candidate suitability based on predictive modeling. AI automates employee onboarding, training programs, and performance management, ensuring a seamless HR workflow. These AI-driven solutions help businesses scale their workforce efficiently while maintaining a high-quality hiring process.

AI-driven financial automation optimizes accounting, invoicing, and fraud detection. Platforms like QuickBooks and Xero use AI to automate bookkeeping, reducing manual data entry and improving financial accuracy. AI-powered fraud detection systems analyze transaction patterns to identify suspicious activities in real time, protecting businesses from security threats. Automated financial reporting provides real-time insights into cash flow, profitability, and expenses, enabling smarter financial decision-making.

By integrating AI into business processes, companies can automate time-consuming tasks, improve decision-making, and scale operations efficiently. The key to successful AI-driven automation lies in selecting the right tools, continuously optimizing workflows, and balancing automation with human oversight. Businesses that embrace AI-powered automation gain a competitive advantage by increasing productivity, enhancing customer experiences, and driving long-term growth.

Scaling AI Content Creation Without Sacrificing Quality

AI has revolutionized content creation, enabling businesses and creators to produce large volumes of high-quality material in less time. However, scaling AI-generated content without compromising authenticity, engagement, and accuracy requires a strategic approach. The key lies in balancing automation with human oversight, refining AI-generated outputs, and leveraging AI tools effectively to maintain consistency and originality.

One of the most effective ways to scale AI content while preserving quality is through structured workflows. AI-powered writing assistants like Jasper, ChatGPT, and Copy.ai can generate blog posts, marketing copy, and social media content rapidly, but human refinement ensures that the output aligns with brand voice and messaging. Implementing a review process where AI drafts content and human editors refine it helps maintain authenticity while maximizing efficiency.

AI-driven content curation and personalization enhance scalability without losing relevance. AI tools analyze audience behavior, engagement metrics, and search trends to generate highly targeted content. Platforms like Clearscope and MarketMuse optimize AI-generated text for SEO, ensuring that content ranks well while remaining informative and engaging. AI-powered analytics track performance and adjust strategies to keep content fresh and valuable for the audience.

Maintaining diversity in AI-generated content prevents it from becoming repetitive or generic. AI models tend to follow patterns, so incorporating human creativity ensures variety in tone, style, and storytelling. Using AI for ideation—such as brainstorming headlines, structuring outlines, or suggesting content formats—while allowing human writers to refine narratives results in high-quality, engaging content.

AI-powered automation also streamlines content repurposing, allowing businesses to scale without overproducing redundant material. AI tools can transform long-form content into bite-sized social media posts, infographics, video scripts, and email newsletters. Video AI platforms like Runway and Synthesia automate video content creation, while AI-driven transcription services convert audio content into blog posts or reports. This multi-channel approach extends content reach without requiring additional manual effort.

Quality control remains essential when scaling AI-generated content. AI-powered grammar checkers like Grammarly and Hemingway ensure readability, while plagiarism detection tools like Copyscape verify originality. AI sentiment analysis tools assess audience reactions, allowing content creators to refine messaging based on user feedback. Maintaining a high editorial standard ensures that scaled content retains credibility, accuracy, and engagement.

By leveraging AI as an assistant rather than a replacement, businesses and creators can scale content production without sacrificing quality. Combining AI efficiency with human creativity, rigorous editing, and strategic repurposing ensures that content remains compelling, relevant, and valuable. AI-driven scalability is not about producing more content for the sake of volume but about maintaining consistency, authenticity, and engagement while reaching a wider audience.

AI and the Future of Entrepreneurship: Opportunities & Risks

Artificial intelligence is reshaping entrepreneurship, providing new opportunities for innovation, efficiency, and scalability. AI-driven automation, predictive analytics, and content generation empower businesses to streamline operations, reduce costs, and enhance decision-making. However, along with these benefits come challenges such as ethical concerns, market competition, and reliance on AI-driven systems. Understanding both the opportunities and risks allows entrepreneurs to harness AI effectively while mitigating potential downsides.

One of the biggest opportunities AI presents for entrepreneurs is automation. AI-powered tools handle repetitive tasks such as customer support, data analysis, content creation, and financial management, allowing business owners to focus on strategy and growth. AI chatbots like Drift and ManyChat provide 24/7 customer engagement, reducing response times and improving customer satisfaction. AI-driven accounting software like QuickBooks automates bookkeeping and financial reporting, saving time and minimizing errors. By integrating AI-driven automation, businesses can scale operations with minimal overhead.

AI enhances decision-making by analyzing vast amounts of data to identify trends, predict consumer behavior, and optimize business strategies. Predictive analytics tools like IBM Watson and Tableau help entrepreneurs make data-driven choices, from market entry strategies to pricing models. AI-powered sentiment analysis enables businesses to monitor customer feedback and adjust products or marketing strategies based on real-time insights. This level of precision helps startups gain a competitive advantage by making informed, data-backed decisions.

AI-driven personalization offers another major advantage for entrepreneurs, particularly in e-commerce and digital marketing. AI recommendation engines analyze customer preferences to deliver personalized product suggestions, increasing conversions and customer loyalty. AI-generated email marketing and ad campaigns tailor messages to individual consumers, optimizing engagement and sales. Businesses that leverage AI to enhance user experiences can drive higher retention rates and stronger brand loyalty.

Despite these opportunities, AI also presents risks that entrepreneurs must consider. One of the main challenges is dependency on AI-driven systems. Businesses that rely too heavily on AI for decision-making or customer interactions may struggle if algorithms fail, data is inaccurate, or AI-generated content lacks authenticity. Ensuring a balance between AI automation and human oversight is crucial for maintaining brand credibility and customer trust.

Ethical concerns surrounding AI in entrepreneurship include data privacy, bias, and job displacement. AI-driven businesses must comply with data protection laws to ensure consumer information is handled responsibly. AI models trained on biased data may produce skewed recommendations or discriminatory outcomes, which can harm brand reputation. Additionally, automation may reduce the need for human labor in certain roles, leading to workforce challenges and ethical considerations about job displacement. Entrepreneurs must navigate these issues carefully to build sustainable and responsible AI-driven businesses.

Market saturation is another risk, as AI makes it easier for entrepreneurs to enter highly competitive industries. With AI-generated content, automated ad campaigns, and AI-driven business models becoming the norm, differentiation becomes more challenging. Entrepreneurs must focus on brand identity, unique value propositions, and strategic positioning to stand out in an AI-driven market.

The future of entrepreneurship will be defined by how well businesses integrate AI while maintaining innovation, ethical responsibility, and human creativity. Entrepreneurs who embrace AI as a tool for efficiency and personalization while addressing risks such as dependency, bias, and competition will thrive in an evolving digital economy. By leveraging AI strategically, businesses can unlock new opportunities for growth, scale operations efficiently, and navigate the challenges of an increasingly AI-driven marketplace.

Final Thoughts: Becoming an AI-Powered Content Mogul

Mastering AI-driven content creation is not just about automation—it's about strategy, creativity, and leveraging technology to build influence, engagement, and revenue. AI provides the tools to generate high-quality content at scale, optimize audience targeting, and personalize messaging, but true success comes from combining AI efficiency with human insight. The future belongs to those who understand how to integrate AI into their content workflows without sacrificing originality or authenticity.

Becoming an AI-powered content mogul starts with choosing the right tools. AI writing assistants, video and image generators, social media automation, and predictive analytics help streamline content production and maximize impact. Platforms like ChatGPT, Jasper, MidJourney, and Runway AI allow creators to generate professional content quickly, but human refinement ensures that content remains engaging and aligned with brand identity. AI should be a collaborator, enhancing creativity rather than replacing it.

Scaling content creation with AI requires consistency and adaptability. AI enables the production of blogs, videos, podcasts, and social media posts at a pace that manual creation cannot match. However, success comes from maintaining a strategic content calendar, analyzing performance data, and continuously refining output based on audience engagement. AI-powered analytics tools track trends, identify high-performing content, and provide insights that inform future strategies.

Monetization is a crucial aspect of becoming an AI-powered content mogul. AI streamlines revenue generation through affiliate marketing, AI-enhanced online courses, digital product sales, and AI-driven ad campaigns. Entrepreneurs who effectively integrate AI into their monetization strategies create scalable income streams while maintaining a strong online presence. AI-powered personalization increases conversions, ensuring content resonates with the right audiences at the right time.

Building authority and trust in an AI-driven content empire requires transparency and ethical considerations. While AI generates content efficiently, maintaining human oversight, ensuring originality, and avoiding over-reliance on automation are essential for credibility. The most successful content creators balance AI efficiency with personal insights, storytelling, and authenticity, reinforcing their brand identity in a competitive digital landscape.

The future of content creation is AI-enhanced, and those who master AI-powered tools while maintaining a human touch will dominate the industry. By combining automation, strategic branding, and audience engagement, content creators can establish themselves as industry leaders. Becoming an AI-powered content mogul is about leveraging technology to scale, optimize, and innovate—turning AI-driven content into influence, impact, and long-term success.

Conclusion

Conclusion: Embracing AI to Build a Future-Proof Content Empire

AI is no longer just a tool for automation—it is a transformative force reshaping content creation, marketing, and entrepreneurship. Those who embrace AI strategically can scale their influence, streamline workflows, and unlock new opportunities for monetization and audience engagement. However, success in an AI-driven landscape requires more than just automation; it demands a balance between efficiency, authenticity, and innovation.

Throughout this book, we have explored how AI enhances content creation, from writing and video production to branding and social media growth. We've seen how AI can predict viral trends, personalize audience interactions, and optimize marketing strategies. More importantly, we've discussed how to use AI responsibly—avoiding bias, maintaining originality, and ensuring content remains high-quality and engaging. The key takeaway is that AI is an enabler, not a replacement for creativity. The best results come from those who use AI to enhance their unique voice, insights, and storytelling rather than relying on it entirely.

As AI continues to evolve, the landscape of digital content and entrepreneurship will shift even further. New tools, platforms, and innovations will emerge, offering greater capabilities for automation, personalization, and business growth. The content moguls of the future will not be those who fear AI but those who master it—leveraging it to maximize efficiency while preserving the human elements that make content compelling.

The future belongs to those who adapt, innovate, and harness AI to build sustainable, scalable, and profitable content-driven businesses. Whether you are an entrepreneur, influencer, or digital creator, your success in an AI-powered world depends on how well you integrate technology with creativity. By staying ahead of trends, refining strategies based on data-driven insights, and continuously improving your craft, you can establish a dominant presence in your industry.

AI is a powerful ally in content creation and business growth, but ultimately, your vision, creativity, and strategic execution will set you apart. Embrace AI, refine your approach, and take action—because the future of content belongs to those who are bold enough to innovate.

References

Books & Academic Papers

1. Agrawal, A., Gans, J., & Goldfarb, A. (2018). *Prediction Machines: The Simple Economics of Artificial Intelligence.* Harvard Business Review Press.

2. Brynjolfsson, E., & McAfee, A. (2017). *Machine, Platform, Crowd: Harnessing Our Digital Future.* W. W. Norton & Company.

3. Russell, S., & Norvig, P. (2021). *Artificial Intelligence: A Modern Approach (4th ed.).* Pearson.

4. Ford, M. (2015). *Rise of the Robots: Technology and the Threat of a Jobless Future.* Basic Books.

5. Haenlein, M., & Kaplan, A. (2019). "A Brief History of Artificial Intelligence: On the Past, Present, and Future of Artificial Intelligence." *California Management Review*, 61(4), 5–14.

AI Tools & Platforms Referenced

6. OpenAI – ChatGPT, DALL·E (https://openai.com)

7. Jasper AI – AI-powered copywriting (https://www.jasper.ai)

8. Copy.ai – AI marketing content generator (https://www.copy.ai)

9. MidJourney – AI-generated artistic imagery (https://www.midjourney.com)

10. Runway ML – AI-powered video editing (https://runwayml.com)

11. ElevenLabs – AI voice synthesis and text-to-speech (https://elevenlabs.io)

12. Murf AI – AI voiceover generation (https://www.murf.ai)

13. Unbounce – AI landing page optimization (https://unbounce.com)

14. Surfer SEO – AI content optimization for search engines (https://surferseo.com)

15. HubSpot – AI-powered marketing automation (https://www.hubspot.com)

Industry Reports & Articles

16. McKinsey & Company (2023). *The State of AI in 2023: Generative AI's Breakout Year.* (https://www.mckinsey.com)

17. Forbes Technology Council (2023). "How AI Is Changing Content Marketing." *Forbes* (https://www.forbes.com)

18. Gartner (2023). *Top AI Trends Shaping Digital Business.* (https://www.gartner.com)

19. Harvard Business Review (2022). "How AI Is Reshaping Marketing and Personalization." (https://hbr.org)

20. PwC (2023). *AI and the Future of Work: Opportunities and Risks.* (https://www.pwc.com)

About the Author

Oliver Grant

Oliver Grant is a futurist, digital strategist, and AI-driven content creator with a passion for merging artificial intelligence with human creativity. With over 15 years of experience in content marketing, automation, and online business development, Oliver has helped entrepreneurs, influencers, and brands harness the power of AI to scale their reach, boost engagement, and create sustainable income streams.

A former software engineer turned AI consultant, Oliver has worked with top-tier tech companies, digital agencies, and startups to develop AI-powered solutions for content generation, social media growth, and marketing automation. His expertise lies in simplifying complex AI tools and making them accessible for writers, marketers, and business owners looking to stay ahead in the rapidly evolving digital landscape.

As the author of *AI-Powered Content Mastery: How to Use Generative AI to Write, Automate, and Grow Your Brand*, *AI Content Revolution: Automate Writing, Marketing, and Passive Income Streams*, and *The Generative AI Playbook: Create Viral Content, Boost Engagement, and Monetize Your Creativity*, Oliver provides actionable strategies to help readers leverage AI for content creation, automation, and brand growth.

When he's not exploring the latest AI innovations, Oliver enjoys mentoring digital entrepreneurs, speaking at industry conferences, and experimenting with AI-generated storytelling. He currently resides in San Francisco, where he continues to push the boundaries of AI-driven creativity and digital business transformation.

Disclaimer

The information presented in this book is for educational and informational purposes only and is not intended as professional advice. The author and publisher have made every effort to ensure the accuracy of the information; however, they assume no responsibility for errors, omissions, or any outcomes resulting from the application of the contents. Readers are encouraged to consult with a qualified professional for specific advice tailored to their situation.

All opinions expressed are those of the author and do not reflect the views of any affiliated organizations. The reader assumes all risks for the use of the material provided in this book. The author and publisher disclaim any liability for direct or indirect consequences arising from the use or interpretation of the information.

Copyright

Legal Notice

This book is for informational and educational purposes only. While the author and publisher have made every effort to provide accurate and up-to-date information, they assume no responsibility for any errors, inaccuracies, or omissions. Any reliance placed on the information in this book is strictly at the reader's discretion and risk.

The content is not intended to replace professional advice, including but not limited to medical, legal, financial, or other professional services. Readers should consult with an appropriate professional for specific guidance related to their unique circumstances.

All trademarks, product names, and company names mentioned herein are the property of their respective owners. Their inclusion does not imply endorsement, affiliation, or sponsorship.

Unauthorized reproduction, distribution, or transmission of this publication in any form is prohibited without prior written consent from the author or publisher.

By reading this book, you agree to indemnify and hold harmless the author, publisher, and any affiliated parties from and against all claims, liabilities, losses, or damages resulting from your use of the information provided.

www.ingramcontent.com/pod-product-compliance
Lightning Source LLC
LaVergne TN
LVHW051742050326
832903LV00029B/2670